Uncertain Promise

An Anthology
of Short Fiction and Creative Nonfiction

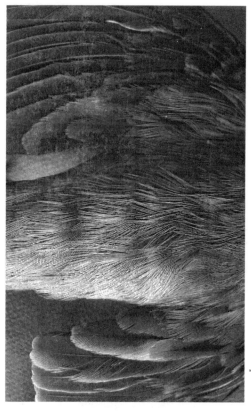

Von Pittman, Editor

© 2014 Compass Flower Press

First publication rights granted to AKA-Publishing / Compass Flower Press by the authors.

Uncertain Promise,
An Anthology of Short Fiction and Non-Fiction

AKA-Publishing / Compass Flower Press does not hold future rights to works included in this volume, however, reprinting, scanning or otherwise copying material in this collection is prohibited except by permission of the author.

ISBN 978-1-942168-01-0

Compass Flower Press
315 Bernadette Dr. Ste 3
Columbia MO 65203
CompassFlowerPress.com

Table of Contents

Introduction – Von Pittman

1	Body Language – First Place – David G. Collins
11	Our Ventana – Second Place – Mary Pacifico Curtis
21	Ballerina – Third Place (tie) – Sally Whitney
27	The Broom – Third Place (tie) – Marlene Lee
33	An Accidental Meeting – Barbara Bagwell
45	Begin Anew – Nidhi Khosla
57	Blame and Shame – Terri Elders
67	A Young Woman of Promise – Elaine Stewart
79	Fahrenheit Meets Celsius – Lori Younker
89	Darwin's Daughter – C. N. Rowland
99	A Time for Joy – Joshua Rigsby
105	Break a Leg – Terry Cobb
111	Coast to Coast – Ramona Scarborough
117	Divergent Directions – William A. Wolff
129	Flight – Lili Flanders
135	Rabbits – Jan Bowman
145	The Poetry Bureau – Kit Salter
155	A Blessing – Berta Rosenberg
165	Some Kind of Royalty – Ida Bettis Fogle
177	Sledding – Kenneth Wise
187	Manatee Mornings – Susan Clements
201	The Decision – Wayne P. Anderson

Introduction

Von Pittman

When Yolanda Ciolli and I began to talk about compiling this anthology, we wondered about the quality that W. Somerset Maugham called "a unity of impression." What would be the collective theme of the stories selected for this collection? After a great deal of lively discussion, we chose "uncertain promise." We believed this theme would not only allow for a great diversity of approaches to storytelling, it should provoke one. The volume and range of responses to our call for submissions certainly justified the choice of theme.

No limits apply on the variety and intensity of promises. We make promises constantly. Usually we do so freely, cheerfully, and without misgivings. We make most of our promises to the important people in our lives—children, parents, lovers, spouses, the people we work with, and even those who are no longer with us. And for the most part, we make them with the best of intentions.

We also make promises to ourselves, pledges that frequently lack certainty. This book includes several stories in which the characters struggle to realize promises they made to themselves. For some, their goals are well defined and achievable. For others, their struggle to keep promises never ends. Some of the promises in these selected stories are fraught with uncertainty, tentativeness, and highly charged emotions. Other promises lead to intense satisfaction, pleasure, or passion. The characters in these stories—fictional and nonfictional—encounter a large variety of emotions, positive and negative.

Yolanda and I wanted to produce a book that would both draw entries from across the country and give writers in our community and state an opportunity to reach a larger audience. We set up an editorial committee that included successful local writers. We divided them into two panels, which made it possible for all local writers to enter. This enabled the shifting of an entry to the other panel, if for example, someone on the first panel had seen the story earlier in a local workshop or critique group. It also made it possible for members of the editorial committees to enter the competition. Their work was simply directed to the other panel.

The members of the editorial committee read all entries "blind." Throughout the entire reading and selections process, neither the members of the editorial committee nor I ever had access to authors' names. We learned their names only after ranking the stories and selecting the winning entries.

The four prizewinning writers covered a range of causes and effects of uncertain promises. In his powerful nonfiction piece, "Body Language," First Prize winner Dave Collins uses a jazz performance to frame his perception of music as a creator of kinetic sensations that both lead and reflect major developments in his narrator's life. Mary Curtis, in "Our Ventana," which took Second Prize, tells a story of lovers on the cusp of a serious relationship, dealing with the lingering presence of a mystical—but real—third person. Marlene Lee and Sally Whitney tied for Third Prize with widely differing stories about the complex—and emotionally dangerous—uncertain promises that accompany rapidly changing relationships.

Other stories involve the promises young people make to themselves, and then must struggle to fulfill, the joyful release from promise to others, and the enduring struggles involved in maintaining commitments to families. This anthology includes a true diversity of approaches inherent in uncertain promises.

Publisher Yolanda Ciolli not only decided to create this collection, but committed herself to producing a product of the highest quality. She deserves the thanks of the entire arts community in our city and region. The members of the Editorial Committees not only exercised acute judgments, they demonstrated an unusual—and highly appreciated—commitment to timelines. Dominique Feldman, AKA-Publishing's intern, kept the vast amount of paperwork flowing in the right directions. Finally, everyone involved in the project would like to thank the anonymous donors who made it possible to offer the extremely generous awards that attracted the efforts of many highly talented and accomplished writers.

Von Pittman, Editor

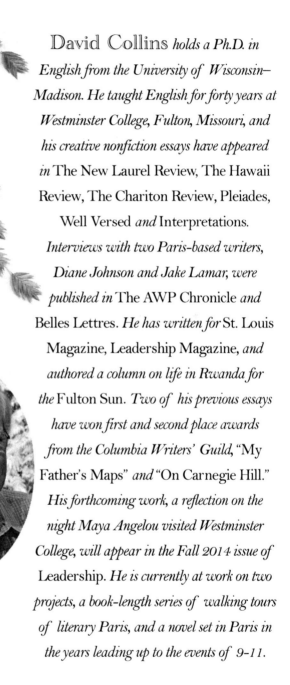

David Collins *holds a Ph.D. in English from the University of Wisconsin–Madison. He taught English for forty years at Westminster College, Fulton, Missouri, and his creative nonfiction essays have appeared in* The New Laurel Review, The Hawaii Review, The Chariton Review, Pleiades, Well Versed *and* Interpretations. *Interviews with two Paris-based writers, Diane Johnson and Jake Lamar, were published in* The AWP Chronicle *and* Belles Lettres. *He has written for* St. Louis Magazine, Leadership Magazine, *and authored a column on life in Rwanda for the* Fulton Sun. *Two of his previous essays have won first and second place awards from the Columbia Writers' Guild, "My Father's Maps" and "On Carnegie Hill." His forthcoming work, a reflection on the night Maya Angelou visited Westminster College, will appear in the Fall 2014 issue of* Leadership. *He is currently at work on two projects, a book-length series of walking tours of literary Paris, and a novel set in Paris in the years leading up to the events of 9-11.*

First Place

Body Language

David G. Collins

Creative Nonfiction

"I was as tall at eleven as I am now. Even then I could pass for twenty-one and play the club scene." Joanne Brackeen is on her feet, towering over thirty or so of the faithful who have gathered to hear about her life as a woman in the male world of jazz. A piano player myself, my eyes go instinctively to her fingers—long, slim, even bony, wiry and strong from constant use like the fingers of a woman I knew who taught deaf children and signed to them for hours each day. My right hand stretches, an unconscious reaction, fingers reaching across keys that aren't there. No comparison. Her reach exceeds mine by two keys, maybe three. Was she really, I wonder, able to pass for twenty-one and to play club dates at an age when I was stumbling through elementary chord progressions? Part of me drifts away to ponder the remembrance of things past, the tricks memory plays, the things we choose to believe, perhaps the things we need to believe about ourselves and how we have become who we are. Another part, much the stronger, is mesmerized by this woman before me.

Brackeen is an arresting figure. Half a foot taller than most women, she meets even a tall man eye to eye. She has borne, I know, three children, but at sixty she carries only as much flesh as is necessary to sustain life. Her body, so obviously full of life, fascinates me. Animated. Full of soul. Standing next to bassist Ray "Bulldog" Drummond—a big man who at dinner tonight will pack two entrées into the cavernous cheeks that have earned him his nickname—further accentuates her sparse frame. When for a moment she stands perfectly still, hands at her sides, a single line rises from her feet to her head. That line suggests to me a sense of unity, an enviable singleness of purpose. Direction. Focus. But such moments of repose are rare for Joanne Brackeen. When she moves, and her body is constantly in motion, she seems all angles, an effect that in another woman might be awkward. Not here. Standing just a few feet away, I can feel the tension, positive energy waiting not so patiently to break out. I can see it in her fingers.

Later tonight, left alone on stage, a moment intended to remind the crowd that the accompanist is himself a master, Ray Drummond will run the changes on Ellington's "Sophisticated Lady," a jazz classic I came to love years ago. Playing it, the hands move every few bars through a succession of rich, full-fingered cords, descending by half tones, steady beat after steady beat, in some of the most harmonically complex passages ever written. I'll lean forward, straining bodily to catch every nuance as Drummond weaves his way through and around the melody, half-revealing, half-concealing the chord progressions that will by the second chorus whisper "Sophisticated Lady" to the *cognoscenti* and leave the unknowing shaking their heads. Though swept away by the percussive intensity of the music that somehow rises from this gentle man, I'll smile as what remains of my conscious mind comes to understand the graceful compliment implicit in his choice. Joanne Brackeen will

Body Language

have left the stage to him, but Drummond's solo, a tribute too subtle to register with many in the crowd, will remind those who know the music that the evening is hers. He is playing tonight with a sophisticated lady and is happy, proud to tell the world as much. Only after the evening's music has passed into memory and emotion has given way to thought will I stop to think of how much I love the succession of seventh, augmented, and diminished cords that give "Sophisticated Lady" its characteristically mournful sound. While Drummond bends over his bass, pressing against, caressing his instrument as if its nearness made him whole, I'll live sensuously in the moment. My only reaction will be the frisson of physical pleasure I've felt so many times as my fingers led my mind through similar passages, passages where I stumble when I think of notes and chords, when I try consciously to direct fingers that know their way by other means.

I came to jazz while still in high school, lured from rock 'n' roll by a friend lucky enough to have parents who knew the music. We listened for hours. We played. From the first I loved the process—a pianist and a chord played again and again, the same notes in different voicings, in different combinations, experimenting later with new notes in substitute chords, listening always for the sound that struck me as "right," the sound that struck the ear "just so." I loved the music, but I was a teenager and, worse yet, a not-so-good Catholic boy restlessly casting about for those magic moments the nuns who drilled me in the Baltimore Catechism deplored as "occasions of sin." My love was far from pure. The funky side of jazz—those moments when Thelonius Monk would slide from the keyboard and plunk his piano's strings, defiantly doing what ought not to be done—carried this would-be rebel to another place. Summer after summer, a devout pilgrim retracing the route to his favorite shrine, I found my way to Newport for the Jazz Festival,

David G. Collins

reveling in the chance to hear three, four, even five legendary players in a single evening. I knew, of course, that the shrine at which I bent my head to pray was a world away from those to which the nuns had sought to lead me. As much as by the music, maybe more, I was lured by the spectacle of the crowd giving itself over to a kind of ecstasy forbidden in the daylight world in which my life seemed then to be spinning away, day by uneventful day. I was lured, too, by the all-night parties that followed on Newport's Second Beach—more music, too much wine, and the much hoped for but, alas, never realized opportunity to get close to a "jazz woman" in a way that would send to their well-worn knees the catechizing nuns who haunted my childhood.

I loved the music because I heard it whispering to me—between notes—the promise of a world beyond the cookie-cutter, suburban ranch house in which I lived, the limits of its well-tended yard marked by a tidy split-rail fence, inhabited and surrounded by ordered, fifties families whose lives in the land of dull tidiness frightened me. Like Langston, who went to Paris and invented jazz poetry, "I thought it was Tangiers I wanted"—or at least the ally behind Hurley's, a bar in Newport where on warm summer nights I would crouch with my underage jazz friends, straining to hear the music over the clatter of dishes from the kitchen as we sipped our under-aged beers in the half-light, or the coffee houses on Thayer Street near Brown University where we snapped our fingers to applaud jazz poets we could barely see through smoke and darkness. I wanted improvisation; I wanted anarchy. Or so I thought.

Watching sports, listening to music, I've for years been aware that I watch in a way others do not. My body moves. Not that I tell it to do anything of the sort. My body moves of its own volition. If I watch a tennis player stretch for a ball, my knees flex, my body leans, my arm reaches for that same ball. If I watch a football player about to take a body-shattering hit, my body tenses up as if I were the one about to be bent in two and smashed to the ground. When I listen to music, truly listen, the rhythms find their way by paths I can't begin to trace into some deep part of me that sets my appendages in motion. Like anyone who has for years been subject to such fits, I know too well the stages by which they come over me. Fingers begin to move of their own accord. One foot escapes my control and begins to tap discretely. Then the other. Soon enough, discretion has been thrown to the winds and my body is in motion from the knees down. If nothing breaks the trance, my head follows, bobbing in time with the music as if percussive accents not pushed along by the thrust of my chin would have no effect. In the final stages my shoulders begin to twitch as well—up and down, back and forth. My grandmother was the first to tell me—and in no uncertain terms—about the sorry figure I cut. "Stop it!" she'd yell. "You look like some poor boy suffering from St. Vitus' Dance." My children, awed and embarrassed, took up her cry years ago. My mouth, they tell me, hangs open when I lose myself at the piano.

Though I may look the fool, I've learned over the years not to worry so much about appearances. I've been amply compensated, like Paul of Tarsus who claimed two thousand years ago that his insights would "destroy the wisdom of the wise" and "bring to nothing the understanding of the prudent." Smug? I suppose. But in moving I've been lessoned. I've learned that art originates in the body, not the mind. I've learned that the arts—far from being effete—are, in fact, muscular. My favorite pianist, the late, much-lamented Oscar Peterson, could coax from his instrument harmonies and melodies guaranteed to dazzle, but when all is said and done the piano is no more than what Ellington and Basie claimed for it long ago—a rhythm instrument. It picks up on, echoes, amplifies and extends, the rhythms of the muscle that sends life pulsing through the body. Jazz begins deep inside with the regular beating of the heart and finds its way out through hands that have will, and memory, and intentions of their own. It's physically conceived before the mind takes over. As is so often the case, the truth lies in the word itself—"jas," the Creole word for dance. When jazz first appeared on the American scene, "jas" was a slang term for sex, the dance of love. "Jazz me." "You can't dance without moving," I told my children, and when I sit at the piano now my body still moves, unashamedly, as the music makes its way through my fingers. I chose jazz for the freedom it promised and I've never been disappointed. I was right. But fifty years at the keyboard have taught me more about jazz, more about life, more about myself. I realize now that I was also wrong. You can't dance—not in any way that makes sense to me—without patterned, regulated movement.

Brackeen's play list for the night is a mix of original compositions and jazz classics, time-honored proving grounds where jazz musicians test their mettle and dare comparison with past masters. Listening as she makes her way through "Body and Soul," a simple melody made memorable by cord changes that reach deep and touch the heart, lyrics written in the language of longing, I realize with just a bit of a shock how much my listening taste inclines both to the old standards and to music that moves slowly. Anyone with a bit of technique can play fast. To play slowly and well demands much more. Joanne Brackeen has learned well the lesson Miles taught before he left—that more notes aren't necessarily better. It's a lesson I'm still learning. Though I love to listen as those who know play with a reserve born of confidence, I can't do it myself. Too afraid, I suppose, that I'll stumble into the dark, silent spaces between the notes and lose my way. And so when in the second set Brackeen turns to her own and Ray Drummond's compositions, all up-tempo on this occasion, I'm an easy mark. This is music I can learn from. And learn I do—but lessons I could not predict, lessons I did not expect. The best kinds of lessons.

I choose my seat for the evening as I do any time the opportunity presents itself, a spot from which I can see the pianist's hands at work. Deep inside I'm hoping for some miracle of sympathetic magic, hoping that seeing will become doing. But what I see and hear is so infinitely beyond anything that might come from my fingers that I'm dazzled. If Joanne Brackeen is an arresting figure when she stands, she's all the more so when seated before a piano. Her playing is dynamic, almost incendiary, her musical energy nothing short of explosive. Barely a minute into the aptly named "Wave" I'm swept away by its propulsive, syncopated rhythms, struck dumb by the sound of rich, full-fingered chords alternating with passages in which Brackeen's fingers run the keyboard with an agility that is nothing if not athletic. Two minutes of listening to her hard-driving, percussive piano, those "fascinatin' rhythms," and my autonomic nervous system has once again kicked in. I'm moving against my will—arms and legs, feet, shoulders, head—dancing in place, a slave to that reptilian brain I wouldn't for a second give up. There's no help for it. The arts *are* muscular and the pleasures they bring *are* physical.

Later in the program I witness—better, I become a part of—one of those moments you live for if the jazz thing has worked its way deep into who you are. The song is Ray Drummond's tribute to his daughter, "Maya's Dance," a title that seems made for this night. Drummond has gathered the base so close to his body that the two seem wrapped in a mutual embrace. His body is bent slightly to the right, his head more so; his eyes are fixed on the pianist feeding him the chords, leading as he follows willingly along. Though Brackeen is seated at the piano, five or six feet away, their bodies are moving together. Dancing. They trade fours and the air crackles with energy that has become synergy, a perfect rapport that has me grinning with delight and all but lifts me out of my seat. When they come together again, my eyes are drawn momentarily to the sight of Drummond's fingers racing dizzily up and down and

David G. Collins

across the strings. But my ears are drawn to Brackeen, hammering at the piano with her trademark two-fisted technique, a kind of barely controlled ferocity that momentarily suggests complete abandon. For a moment I hear the freedom I sought as a teenager. The sound rolls and builds, bouncing from floor to ceiling and from wall to wall in a very live room, rolls and builds and rolls and builds. And then—more suddenly, more "at once" than I would ever have believed possible—both musicians stop. They stop dead and the silence hangs in the air. How long? A second? Two seconds? Three? What breaks the spell is an audible, collective gasp of disbelief from the audience. How did they do it? How did they come out of a frantic, free-flowing improvisation and stop so completely together?

Like everyone else, I had been moving, moving, looking for the next note, startled when it didn't come, aghast at what had been withheld and at the suddenness of the withholding. What others felt when the music stopped I don't know. I felt chastened. I felt as though I had asked for too much, as though I had behaved badly by wanting more. A whining schoolboy again, scolded for self-indulgence. Far in the back of my mind, tucked away, obscured for the moment by what I felt, I sensed the hint of an idea, felt it as surely as I felt the music seconds earlier. Unformed as yet, indecipherable, I knew that as I calmed down and turned away it would rise to consciousness. But before it could assume any shape I recognized, the music began again and I was swept away to that familiar place where intuitive appreciation is all that matters. Brackeen had thrown herself into "Cram 'n' Exam," a bebop piece written for her students at the New England Conservatory of Music. Once again I'm awed by the profusion of her musical ideas, none pursued for more than a few bars before giving way to another. Then it happens again. Once more the sound rolls and builds; the room comes alive as hard struck chord follows hard struck chord. Everyone knows the climax is coming. From where I'm sitting I can see Brackeen's

Body Language

hands in that last moment, poised over the keys, those long fingers spread wide, ready to crash decisively on one final chord. But to my surprise, her hands never come down. Something passed between pianist and bassist, the slightest look, the slightest movement of a body, and her hands hung there, suspended over the keyboard. Drummond took the last note and, suddenly, the rest was silence.

As the silence rose around me, I realized that I had somehow come to understand what had eluded me earlier. Joanne Brackeen had chosen those last notes, knew in her mind what she was going to do to close out "Cram 'n' Exam." Did she think better of it? Or did those muscular fingers, guided by some most subtle sign, some language of the body known only to those in the innermost circle, choose for her? My money—no surprise—is on the fingers and the muscles that move them, muscles that need no mind to tell them what to do or, as I've suddenly come to realize is more important, what *not* to do. I know better now, fifty years and more after first discovering jazz, why I want to live in this music. I chose once because I found jazz ferocious, anarchic, a deliverance from the buttoned-down, daylight life to which I had been born. I mistook, but I'm not sorry. My mis-taking served me well through five decades as I found in jazz what I needed.

But my needs now are different. One person can make jazz, but I like it best as a collaboration, a negotiation between two, or three, or more. I've come to realize that where there are many, no one can have absolute freedom. What matters is control within freedom, restraint, knowing when to hold back that note, when to stop so absolutely together that the audience is astounded. I've learned to listen better now, learned to watch the bodies talking.

Mary Pacifico Curtis

Mary's poetry and prose have been published by LOST Magazine, The Rumpus, The Boston Literary Magazine, the Naugatuck River Review, the Pitkin Review, Calyx *and* The Crab Orchard Review. *Anthologized work includes the* Las Positas Literary Anthology, The Times They Were A'Changin' *and* The Widows Handbook. *When not writing, Mary leads a Silicon Valley life as CEO of Pacifico Inc, a PR and branding firm, and as a venture angel to tech startups.*

Second Place

Our Ventana

Mary Curtis

Creative Nonfiction

The day begins with sunshine and soft breezes, a proclamation of spring out of season in what should be a California winter. Neither of us has slept well, perhaps because of a bad chianti, a salty meal or some unsettled expectation of the weekend. After morning routines, we load backpacks into the car and take off with the convertible top down. En route, I call a daughter, change theater tickets and check travel details for an overnight trip next week. I have worried about this weekend because he wants to take me to the place where your ashes are buried. Though the conversation is mundane, I feel myself retreating into a sense of reverence for the unknown to come. Turning onto the road to the coast, our conversation slows as we pass artichoke fields and the occasional trailer park.

Mary Pacifico Curtis

In photos, your face is round with auburn hair and many looks. Sometimes the hair is pulled straight back in simplicity that shows large brown eyes, a smile that belies both reserve and willingness to enter the moment. Other times the hair cascades around your shoulders in large curls, a length and softness often stereotyped as ultra-feminine. Still other times, you have light bangs and somehow look more Latina, as if the shadows cast by your hair darken skin and eyes.

And there are your characters—Carmen Miranda *in a headdress that is abundant with tropical fruit, and the tapered dress scantly draping a curvaceous body.* Diana *in* Chorus Line, Sally Bowles *in* Cabaret, Mazeppa *in* Gypsy. *Once I wondered what your voice sounded like, and listened to the recording of the "Counting Song" from RapMaster Ronnie. Those who know say that in your day you were a triple threat—acting, singing and dancing onstage all the while teaching your 'kids,' and later choreographing shows on cruise ships.*

We pass through busy Monterey traffic, merge into the narrowing road through Carmel, and push on to our destination in Big Sur.

Just last night he told me you selected the place where your ashes would be buried—the place called Ventana which means "window"—and you specified a small pond with the ocean beyond.

He has told me of his solo trip there last year, of the many bird feeders that people have brought to the clearing where, three years ago, he traveled with family and friends to conduct a memorial, bury your ashes and honor your wish to be in the place where your spirit would "pass through the window." He showed me the photo of your name as he traced it in the dirt with twigs, and spoke in happy tones about the many hummingbirds that are drawn to the place.

Our Ventana

After some brief chatter about the bank of fog stretching inland to the coastal mountains, and the proximity of the Continental Shelf to Carmel Beach soon behind us on the right, I ask, "Was that her personality, to organize and direct things like she did her own memorial?"

I have come to know your house—the chairs where you sat, the bed where you slept and made love, your desk and its display of miniature Buddhas you collected. I have looked through your books on shamanic practices, curative Chinese recipes, the history of Broadway, Toltec practice, and healing with the five elements. I have stood in silent reverie looking at your crystals, feathers and rattles—inspirations and remedies of the shaman you became. Your house was tidy—a reflection of a life lived on the move, and later kept in readiness for people who came to you for healing and bodywork.

Television played throughout the day when you were home alone, yet you were an avid reader. You loved movies but hated violence, and would walk out to read in the theater lobby. You loved a good hotel room and were not much of a camper. You lost a pregnancy and nearly your life. I'm told you did not identify yourself as a mother type anyway. You lived close to your sister, and maintained strong relationships with hundreds of cousins, uncles and aunts. You entertained on a wooden platform built low to the ground encircling a huge avocado tree that shaded most of your back yard. I know all of this from your husband.

"No," he answers considering the anomaly. "No, in fact the opposite. She was pretty far along in her Shamanic work by the time she became ill, and she was very comfortable with what she knew of 'the other side.' I'm not sure how hard she fought or if she felt attached to this life."

He has said this before.

Uncertain Promise

The two of you kissed early on your first date at a Neville Brothers concert and he was certain you would have a life together. By that time, both of you had come through marriages to spouses who had been unfaithful. You produced shows on cruise ships together, moved across country, and you transitioned from performing to choreography and then to the healing arts. His job took you back to the west coast—nearer to your mother and a nephew who battled cancer—one would survive, one would succumb..

Telling your husband that he did not get a vote since he was never home, you got a dog. You trained the dog impeccably. You lost your dancer's trimness and said you wanted to lose ten pounds. You were a devoted wife to a husband who often worked long hours and nights. You trusted him and he was faithful and adoring. The pictures from that time show a thoroughly comfortable married couple. You traveled less and were alone more. You were close to immediate family in the way that relatives come together and push apart. I do not know who your friends were. I wonder how lonely you were, and if you spoke of it.

You were peace-loving and non-confrontational—seemingly not at all jealous, possessive, or insecure. You eschewed business and have been credited with making art in all you undertook. You didn't have a temper; you had chronic fatigue syndrome. You didn't make a practice of rigorous exercise; you walked. You made plans to move again, and start a business together; you were diagnosed.

"She worked with her healer down here and her other healers on her plan for her ashes."

Patches of murk and shine mottle the grey ocean simmering under vaporous cloud. As the road pitches between north facing and south facing turns, we slow behind drivers who brake constantly as if a steady speed would be dangerous. Minutes later a waning sun breaks through, white-lighting western facing trunks, branches and detritus of towering eucalyptus trees.

Our Ventana

I have stepped into a space that you vacated, becoming friend, lover, and mate to the man you left behind.

We are at a new moment, in our odd way joined—though you will never know me—never look into my green eyes nor I into your brown ones in a conversation that reveals our differences and similarities. We have an unfortunate convergence: my birthday is one day before the anniversary of your death.

I have thought all these thoughts in the months, weeks, and days before this weekend, one in which he and I will travel to Big Sur. We have billed it to friends who know the ironic coupling of these days as a "celebration of life"—both mine and yours.

We continue in silence, soon reaching the roadside inn where we will spend the night. After check-in and inspection of our modest oak paneled room, we are back in the car.

"Let's go to Nepenthe." He looks at me, already in motion. Only later will I understand Nepenthe as the drug described in Homer's *Odyssey* as banishing troubles or grief.

A short distance later, we pull into a dirt parking lot. "I'd like to get a little something to put there."

He is speaking almost to himself as he locks the car, and then as an afterthought looks at me, "Do you mind if we go to where she is?"

"Not at all." His urgency is palpable.

It is the reason we are here, I think to myself, acknowledging my own colliding feelings. On the one hand, this is their time and their place—and on the other, he has brought us together, the three of us, for reasons yet to be known.

We circle the gift shop finally finding a small tin and wicker rattle, which he pronounces perfect and buys. We walk the stairs to the restaurant and its view of the ocean and Big Sur to the south. Crows cluster in near oak branches and a turkey buzzard circles and circles, waiting for scraps below. Beyond the steep slope from the decks where we stand, I see a brambly barrier to Highway 1 that opens to a green meadow, a small pond, and the ocean beyond.

"That's it." He speaks very quietly at my side. "That's where she is. Just up from the grassy area. She wanted a pond with the ocean."

I have already taken pictures of the turkey vulture in flight, the coastal vista, and the murder of crows. "Take a picture of that, will you? I'd like to send it to a few people."

I frame the spot tight in my viewfinder. Then I turn the camera and take a shot of the two of us. We smile uncertain smiles—my interpretation as I review the photo. I wonder what it will be like to walk in the Ventana meadow below us.

Back in the car, I ask, "What does the rattle mean to you?"

"It's the presence of the spirit. When I came last year I left a little rattle too." A gift—and a call to her spirit.

"The rattles have less meaning for me," he continues. "They're Shamanic symbols for the spirit."

Redwoods and Eucalyptus stretch tall and canopy the road as we reach a turnout just around a bend.

"This is it, but I think we can go in from the other side."

He has slowed and turned off, passing a filthy old Volvo and an equally beat up Chevy van with tie-dye curtains across the windows. Behind the barricade of these vehicles, I glimpse a skinny man of unknowable age silhouetted in tatters, a wild frizz of ponytail and bits of escaped hair with a supersized bottle of beer. I am suddenly very happy to be "going in from the other side."

We soon discover a wide barbed wire gate blocking the path we were hoping to take. It is posted with more "keep out" and "no trespassing" signs, so we walk back to the van and station wagon parked in front of the main trail entrance. Peering around the vehicles, we see another wide gate with "keep out" signs. Standing with the tattered frizz man, a smaller blonde man releases a volume of smoke coloring the eucalyptus air.

"When did they close this off?"

"S'been a while." A yellow-toothed grimace. "They don't want no one in there."

"I've been there. It's a beautiful spot. Just getting too trampled?"

"Yeah, man, just 'magine that you're only one of the ten thousands of people that come here thinkin' it's their spot. Their secret spot." Spoken with another pungent release of smoke that swirls around his head and body, mixing to a golden haze in the dust and sunlight and the curl of his lips on the word "secret."

"Yeah, well, it's a beautiful spot." Wistful, he turns to me, turns to the gate, and takes my hand. "Take care."

We start back to the car.

"That's a shock."

"I don't even know how to feel—how to think about that. It's a big shock." He sounds shaken.

Does he feel as if you have again been ripped out of his life?

I stay quiet—do I console or give him the space to know his feelings? Although I have wondered what to expect in the moments when the three of us would come together in this place, there are different questions now. I have a sense of irony—that death has its final word yet again, denying the resolution he surely intended as he embraces our new life side by side with his old one.

Over the next hours we talk about the irony, the shock of those closed gates and forbidden access—of what it all means. I see that he is letting it roll around in his brain along with the sadness of the day, and whatever unmet expectation he might feel. Over dinner, we chat with an affable waiter about wines and Santa Barbara, living at home after graduating, and plans for medical school. We circle the shock as if by sampling every dimension of our feelings we will find understanding.

"I still don't know how to think about it."

"It feels so ironic to me."

"It's a message of some sort."

"Message?"

"It couldn't have been more clear that access was blocked off—denied." Seconds later he added, "I kind of wanted to say 'when did you get so private'?"

"You must feel disappointed."

"It's not that. I'm not disappointed. I've been ready to let go. I want to understand."

His processing peppers our conversation between stories of their life together and stories shared as our waiter brings dishes and then clears them. I wonder if we will make love, or if the day truly belongs to his memories and the Ventana wilderness. He orders apple pie made famous by the owners of the inn, and is quickly served a large slice with a mound of vanilla ice cream. We make plans to hike, visit coastal art galleries and buy fresh crab the next day. We return to our room and make love with an urgency that we both understand.

In the morning, we step outside to soft breezes and sun filtering through the redwoods. Crossing the road he says, "Let's go to the river after we eat."

Again in the rustic dining room, we linger over oatmeal and coffee.

"What a day yesterday, certainly not what we came here for or expected…" I say. "Do you want to…"

"No, I've been ready—I don't want to go back." He sits up very straight. "That time is over and done. The message could not be more clear—it's time for us, time to go on, our time."

Sally Whitney's *short stories have appeared in literary and commercial magazines, including* Bloodroot Literary Magazine, The Main Street Rag, Kansas City Voices, *and* Pearl, *and anthologies, including* Voices From the Porch, New Lines from the Old Line State: An Anthology of Maryland Writers, *and* Grow Old Along With Me—The Best Is Yet to Be, *among others. The audio version of* Grow Old Along With Me *was a Grammy Award finalist in the Spoken Word or Nonmusical Album category. Whitney's stories were also semi-finalists in the* Syndicated Fiction Project *and the* Salem College National Literary Awards *competition and received honorable mention in the* Shenango River Books Prose Chapbook Contest. *Whitney is a guest blogger for* SheWrites.com *and a regular contributor to* LateLastNightBooks.com. *She lives with her husband in Maryland and is currently working on a novel. Her website is http://www.sally-whitney.com.*

Third Place Tie

Ballerina

Sally Whitney

Fiction

She danced the way she wanted. Each turn of her arms, each bend of her legs was perfect. Harold watched the shimmering of her satin-covered toes and knew she had moved to another plane, another existence. She was what she wanted to be, and it was breath-taking. Harold had never had that moment of complete peace with who he was and what he did, that moment when he heard music that was right for him, and he longed for it. He watched her dance and was awestruck. Such beauty transcended imagination and desire.

The next instant it was over. The music stopped, and the pulsating, vibrant body fell silent. Sweat-drenched, limp, she resembled a dew-covered flower, its petals bending gently toward the ground. "Harold," she said softly, "can you get me a towel?"

Harold startled into reality, seeing the person where once had been the dance. A hasty search revealed a twisted towel heaped in the corner of a chair. He placed it around her shoulders. "Exquisite," he whispered.

She patted his cheek and wiped sweat from her forehead with the towel. "You always say that," she said. His embarrassment made him smile.

They left the studio together as they always did. A rush of bitter, ice-tinged air greeted them outside. They turned up their collars and tightened their mufflers. The world was a glass music box. Each sparkling tree limb reflected the reds and oranges of late afternoon sun, while the breeze created a tinkling melody high in the frozen tree tops. Harold tried to keep his arm around her as they walked down the narrow salted path in the sidewalk, but she darted left and right, laughing at the crunch of the frozen grass.

Harold realized later he should have seen the danger. Like an ogre climbing out of its cave, it should have beckoned to him from the shining steps. In a flash she hopped from the grass to the steps. Her toes flew into the air, and for a second, her graceful arms flailed wildly. Harold reached for her, but she was beyond him. She collapsed into a tight ball on the edge of the slippery steps, her right ankle buried beneath her.

Harold moved toward her carefully. "Are you hurt?" he asked.

"Just my pride."

"Let me help you up." He pulled her to a standing position. She balanced for a moment on her left foot, then stepped gingerly on her right. As her foot made contact with the ground, her face contorted and she cried out.

"I can't walk," she said. He slid one arm underneath her shoulders, the other behind her knees, and prepared for a great lift. To his surprise, she felt almost weightless, a hollow-boned bird under those strong, hard muscles. Harold carried her to the car, stepping deftly around the treacherous patches of ice.

Ballerina

The ankle was fractured. An alabaster doctor applied a pale, heavy cast. Harold arranged the day bed in her apartment with the largest, laciest pillows and the daintiest, softest quilt. He brewed apricot tea and bought lemon tarts at the bakery.

"Stop fussing over me," she said. "Don't you have somewhere you need to be?"

"Maybe later," he said. He ached for her lost wings and blamed himself for allowing her unique beauty to be—temporarily, he prayed—destroyed.

The days, she complained, trudged like oxen in mud. Harold read Shakespeare aloud, hoping to divert her attention with the smooth melodies of the sonnets. When she tired of that he tried Rimsky-Korsakov, but the familiar cadences made her yearn for her satin slippers and the passion that ignited her body.

Finally, in desperation, he created a diversion of his own. Timidly at first, he recorded on paper his feelings about the world, his observations, his reactions, hoping to invite her response. His first poem was three lines long. He wrote it as she slept and he sat beside her. Outside the window on the frozen sill, an abandoned robin pecked forlornly for imagined crumbs or seeds.

"I wonder," Harold wrote, "why we often see only what we want." He left the paper beside her pillow and went out to buy her supper.

When he returned, she sat propped against the pillows. He bent to kiss her nose, and she slipped a piece of paper into his hand. "Read it later," she cautioned, "in private."

That night, alone in his apartment, he unfolded the paper. "Our eyes can be windows," she wrote, "or mirrors reflecting our minds." Harold laughed out loud. He seized a sheet of stationery, located his pen, and began his next work, expanding this time to ten lines. Her response was equally long and revealed a depth of imagination he didn't know she had. Once the pattern was established, they sometimes wrote each other four or five times a week.

Uncertain Promise

To his surprise, Harold never lacked subjects to write about. The snows returned, bringing mountains of cushiony whiteness that often shaped themselves into the foundation of his work. The house plants, wishing for freedom from their close-fitting pots, sang to him. Memories of his childhood, long suppressed because he deemed them worthless, reared their heads and begged for the recognition they deserved. He tried rhymed poetry, free verse, then sonnets. He considered each creation a small offering to her.

She responded for a while. But as the length, depth, and frequency of his work increased, he was writing again before he received an answer.

One day, as he entered her apartment with his latest poem, she stood beside the day bed. The lilting strains of "The Sugar Plum Fairy" floated through the room, and she moved her arms with the grace of the music. Her shoulders swayed in complement to her arms, and occasionally she leaned gently on her casted foot. She didn't see him come in, and he didn't want to frighten her, so he tiptoed to the stereo and turned off the CD. "I brought you a poem," he said. "It's my best one yet."

She half-smiled. "I'm sure it is. I'll read it when I finish this set."

"Will you answer this one?" Harold asked.

Her smile melted. "If I have time," she said.

"Should you be standing on your foot?" A flood of fire poured through Harold's veins.

"It's been six weeks," she said. "I have to get back in practice."

"Too much work could be bad for you." He tossed the poem on the table.

"I know when to stop. If you don't believe me, stay and watch."

Harold sat stiffly on the edge of the day bed. She limped to the stereo and started the CD. The music flowed around her and lured her body. Almost at once her arms, her head, her shoulders moved, seemingly oblivious of the weight on her foot. Harold's anger cooled to a glow as the old magic overtook him. She was magnificent, even restricted.

Ballerina

She wrote no more poems. Harold tried to inspire her with his work, but she responded only with a cool smile and the excuse that she had no time. But Harold could not stop writing. If he could create the right work of art, he could unlock that spark of imagination he had discovered in her and grown to love.

He wrote furiously. The trickling streams of melting snow made music for his sonnets. The purple crocuses gave color to his poems. And one day blue birds flew straight into an essay. He reached out into his world and found that what had only amazed or perplexed him before now made sense in the scratchings on his paper. He saw what he had never seen before and shaped it into more than it alone could be.

By this time, her ankle was healed and the cast removed. She went each day to the studio. Harold came to watch when he could, but he had so little time. There was so much to write.

One afternoon, as they walked home from the studio in a sweet-smelling rain, she asked him, "What do you do with your time now? I hardly see you anymore."

"I write," he said.

"I miss you. I want you near me."

"I'll try harder," Harold said.

The next day he made himself go to the studio early. He took his usual seat on the cold folding chair and waited for her to begin. The music came first, the crashing dissonance of Stravinsky. Then she exploded onto the dance floor, a tumult of energy and art. Harold watched, consumed in the usual awe, until a newly familiar craving crept through his soul.

Silently, he took a paper and pen from his pocket. He turned in his chair and pulled another close to write on. As the dancer and the music became a misty abstraction, the thoughts and words became concrete. He was what he wrote and it was he. He danced the way he wanted.

Marlene Lee has published The Absent Woman, *a novel*, Rebecca's Road, *a short-story collection, and three mystery novellas gathered under the title,* Scoville *with Holland House Books of London, England. Her fourth book,* Limestone Wall, *set in and around the old Missouri State Penitentiary, will be released by Holland House November 1st of this year. Marlene worked for many years as a court reporter. She is a graduate of Kansas Wesleyan University and taught high school English in Salina, Kansas before teaching undergraduate English classes at the University of Kansas and Brooklyn College where she received, respectively, the MA and MFA degrees. She won first and third prizes in the Pacific Northwest Writers Conference novel contest as well as first prize in the University of Kansas Poetry Contest. Her fiction, poems, and essays have appeared in numerous publications.*

Third Place Tie

The Broom

Marlene Lee

Fiction

It was one day before Clara's flight home to New York. She threw a broom in the back of the red pickup truck without explaining why, and climbed into the passenger seat.

"Mind if I drive around a little?" she said to Raymond.

He stopped nursing his toothpick and turned to look at her. "If you wait a minute while I stop by the feed store, I'll drive you wherever you want to go."

She laid her hand on his arm. "It's something I want to do by myself. It's irrational. Just nostalgia." They'd talked about nostalgia the night before. It had bothered both of them to be talking when they'd expected to be making love.

In New York, Clara was considered verbal; here she adopted the local laconic style. "Last night in bed. . ."

"Yup."

". . . do you think we're just tired?"

Raymond leaned forward and checked both directions before turning onto the dirt road that needed blading since the last hard rain. When he'd finished shifting gears, and they were bumping toward Oakley, he leaned back and acted like he'd forgotten what she'd said. She knew he hadn't.

"I'm not tired," he said with a twitch of his right shoulder. "Are you?"

"A little."

"You tired of me?" he said, and looked at the road again.

"No. Are you tired of me?"

"No." The day was beautiful, the blue sky lifting high to make room for the mountains beginning to build here in the plains where Western Kansas steadily rises to erupt in the Rockies a few hours west.

"Do you want me to leave ahead of time?" she asked. She never said "ahead of time" in Manhattan. She must have been pulling words from the part of her mind that had formed when she was learning to talk. She derived comfort from thinking the phrases came directly from her dead mother, etched into a little daughter's impressionable mind, carried forward from Kansas, a legacy.

He reached across and touched her knee. "You mean leave today instead of tomorrow?" The impracticality was obvious. "I'll drop you off"—his forehead lifted a little, not enough to be bad manners, but enough to show he was troubled—"and pick you up on my way back." He knew where she was going. The truck almost stayed in the ruts by itself.

The grain elevator a mile away stood high above the flat wheat and alfalfa fields. So did the steeple of St. Elizabeth of the Plains several miles in the other direction. St. Elizabeth was a German Catholic town. The grain elevator was in the Protestant town, Oakley, where the Methodist and Baptist churches were well attended but didn't assert their architecture.

The Broom

When he turned into her grandparents' abandoned farmyard, she got out and stood on tiptoe to reach the broom in the truck bed.

He smiled. "You planning to sweep the place clean?"

"I guess I'm trying to be a good girl." And that, too, was funny, because they both knew she wasn't.

"Watch for snakes," he reminded her, and then the truck was trailing dust out of the yard and turning onto the road close to where the mailbox used to sit.

She lifted her feet high in the weeds. Above her, the disengaged windmill squeaked and rattled, turning in the wind. The windmill and the stone wash house beside it, the rusted round water tank on top, all had been there while the family passed back and forth below, drank from the well, nudged open the wash house door with a foot while holding a bushel basket of laundry. All were gone. The work they'd done to keep the house and farm from dust, grasshoppers, had been ultimately useless.

The door to the wash house was padlocked shut. No more swishing water, soap smells, shavings from gray soap bars, two rinses, sometimes three for fine goods. No more mother and grandmother, sister, sister-in-law, aunt and great-aunt voices. All had gone away while the windmill turned in the wind and the prairie, neither kind nor malevolent, absorbed the sun and rain.

The cyclone cellar had no padlock. Its long wood doors, slanting upward toward what would have been the outer wall of the house, were splintered and worn away at the corners. The location of the kitchen door, where she used to step out to meet her grandfather carrying pails of milk from the barn past the windmill, up the cement walk, was now brush. The wild growth was already hot this morning, the scent of earth's sweat released. Insects were busy getting food, skittering and flying, buzzing and humming, eating and being eaten in a green, spicy world.

Uncertain Promise

Marlene Lee

With difficulty, she bent down and opened each heavy door. She pulled up and out. One banged to the ground when she lost control. She stared down into the cement stairwell. Stored air traveled up to her, swelling her passages. She'd opened a grave. Damp dirt smell and scent of sour milk penetrated her. Down there is where the separator had been, where the milk was separated from the cream. That's why her grandfather was bringing the pails to this spot, milk and milk foam sloshing over the edges of the metal buckets.

She went back to the wash house where she'd leaned the broom against a leg of the windmill, and carried it to the cellar by its smooth handle. She treasured the simplicity of brooms, buckets, steps into the earth. She bent toward the threshold, picked up the broom, and began sweeping. Corners caked with dirt had to be dug into, struck again and again with stiff bristles. She progressed down each step, delivering topsoil to the bottom. The sour milk smell climbed the steps and passed her on its way up to the prairie. At the last step she swept the accumulated dirt onto the dirt floor, another layer of time added to the cellar. Down here, shelves lined the walls, but the jelly jars and Mason jars of beans, tomatoes, applesauce, pickles were gone. Gone the milk separator. Gone the little puddles of spilled milk the cats licked up. Gone the cats.

She remained motionless for fifteen minutes, and when she came up again and had closed the cellar doors, she felt better than when she'd gone down there, sweeping.

"Did you clean 'er up?" Raymond said after she'd dropped the broom in the truck bed again and climbed up into the passenger seat. He was expressionless. His head settled a doubtful notch closer to his lifted shoulder.

She smiled ruefully. "The cyclone cellar steps have never been cleaner. I saw the shelves and the spot where the milk separator sat."

He ground the gears more than he meant to. "Take that broom

The Broom

back to New York with you." She ignored his meaning.

"I want to show you something," he said. When they got to the place he was going, which was uphill, a rare high spot that the glacier had missed, he got out. "We have to walk from here."

They walked up a rocky hillside. The wind blew from Canada. They felt it pass them on its way south. She began to perspire and ran her hand across her forehead, then beneath her blouse where she wiped away sweat under her breasts. They reached the ridge that seemed high because the land below was so flat.

She looked for landmarks. "Can you see the farm?"

He pointed to the north. "Behind that line of cottonwoods."

Directly below them was the country cemetery where her mother, grandparents, two aunts, and an uncle were buried. His relatives were buried there, too. He followed her gaze. "They're all underground," he said. "You want your broom?"

He took a step closer and put his arm around her shoulders. He held her against his generous body. "You go back and take care of your husband," he said. "That's what will clear your mind."

"I grew up here. I have to come see the land and you."

"You take care of your husband," he repeated. "That's what our trouble is."

"He's not my husband," she said.

"Fifteen years. That's a husband."

Words died in her throat. Her world buckled before it fell into place again. He disengaged himself and began climbing down the hill. She looked at the distant line of cottonwoods, the gravestones below, the grain elevators to the south, the Catholic spire on the horizon. She followed him. Everywhere grass and plants constituting crops moved in the wind.

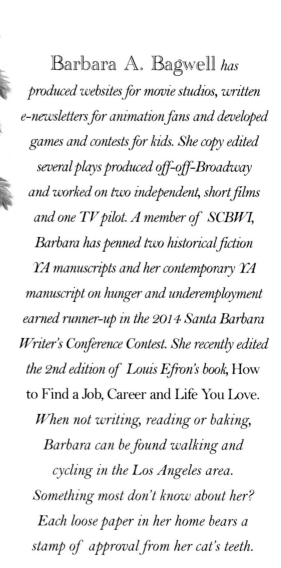

Barbara A. Bagwell *has produced websites for movie studios, written e-newsletters for animation fans and developed games and contests for kids. She copy edited several plays produced off-off-Broadway and worked on two independent, short films and one TV pilot. A member of SCBWI, Barbara has penned two historical fiction YA manuscripts and her contemporary YA manuscript on hunger and underemployment earned runner-up in the 2014 Santa Barbara Writer's Conference Contest. She recently edited the 2nd edition of Louis Efron's book,* How to Find a Job, Career and Life You Love. *When not writing, reading or baking, Barbara can be found walking and cycling in the Los Angeles area. Something most don't know about her? Each loose paper in her home bears a stamp of approval from her cat's teeth.*

Compass Flower Press

An Accidental Meeting

Barbara A. Bagwell

Fiction

"That helmet saved your friend's life." The ER doctor gestured at the cracked helmet gripped in Tracy's hands. "You'll be released, but she must stay in the hospital overnight to monitor her concussion. We must wake her frequently so she won't fall into a coma."

Carmela's tiny form lay still under the white sheet pulled to her chin. Her closed eyes wouldn't stay that way long, if the attending's words meant anything. A blank sort of peace rested on her face.

I knew my own face must reflect relief from the fear surging through me all afternoon. Adrenaline hit my veins once I discovered blood on Carmela's head as she sprawled on the road. Knowing someone from the age of eight makes them sister-material by the time you hit thirty. I wished I could wipe from my memory banks the visual of her out cold on a backboard. Carmela's earlier groggy state made it difficult to tell whether she'd remember anything of the accident. I wished I didn't.

I took a deep breath then released it. This could have been much worse.

A line of stitches and bruises on the left side of Carmela's face did not hide the beautiful, Latin bone structure in her cheeks. Thank God the X-ray showed no broken facial bones.

The image of both my friends flying over the handlebars then smashing the pavement as we plummeted downhill raced across my mind. Several other riders crashed into and over those sprawled on the pavement before I could stop to help. I pushed the images away.

"I'll be back in a bit." The doctor squeezed past me into the rush of the ER. It seemed cyclists in spandex shorts took over this fragment of Denver Hospital. On one side of Carmela's bed, I'd drawn the curtain back to accommodate an ease of conversation between Carmela and Tracy's beds.

I stood between my friends, unable to sit from the adrenaline still pumping through my veins. A man's pair of clunky, cycling clip shoes paced the curtained space beside us. I wondered if he was a buddy to the two men who caused the accident or someone else caught in their mayhem.

Tossing a water balloon down a switchback mountain for fun from a car was one thing, but doing it on a bike surrounded by others guaranteed disaster. Their antics nearly killed my friend.

I shifted the ice pack I held on Tracy's shoulder. She took it, handing me Carmela's cracked helmet with shaking fingers.

"I'll stay with Carmela." Tracy tugged her brunette braid, pulling it out from the sling holding her dislocated shoulder in place. She winced. I eyed the road rash burn down her left thigh. The sticky-sweet smell of antiseptic ointment hit my nose. Her leg shimmered with it.

"We'll both stay," I said.

An Accidental Meeting

"Like hell," Tracy said. "You're finishing the ride for all three of us. Don't give up."

"We're a team, Trace. I'm not giving up. I want to make sure you guys—."

"Excuse me, ladies? Would you happen to know if the unconscious lass be alright?" a man's Irish-accented voice said behind me.

I turned, finding myself eye-to-eye with a man wearing a green, white and orange racing jersey. At five feet, eleven inches, I usually beheld the men around me from above. This man's shoulders dwarfed mine, but his lean frame indicated his avid riding status. Jet black hair rose in spikes over his forehead with a pleasing face and a beak nose.

Tracy's knee nudged me. She moaned after scraping her skin on the stiff sheet. I waved my hand behind my back at her. This was the guy she claimed had a crush on me at the noon rest stop—though we had done nothing more than giggle over Elvis, using a few bananas and some peanut butter sandwiches.

The concern on his face now seemed genuine enough. Perhaps Tracy was wrong? Was Carmela the source of his attention, not me? I forced a smile, but without my dimples. Those only appeared with genuine joy.

"Carmela will be fine," I told him. "Thanks for asking. They'll admit her tonight. You can stop by later when she's awake to tell her your concerns yourself, if you'd like."

The man lifted an eyebrow at me. Amusement tickled his lips. I felt my heart jump. I beat it into submission. I didn't even know his name yet.

"While I hate seeing a beautiful lass in pain, my friend be the one interested in speaking to Miss Carmela. As soon as they issue him crutches, that is."

"Crutches?" Tracy said. "Who needs crutches when your beds rest side-by-side? We're all in spandex shorts; there ain't no modesty here. Tug that curtain open, would you? Like ours."

"Excellent idea," he ducked around the curtain. A murmur of male voices reached us through the pink-striped fabric.

"See, Teagan?" Tracy whispered. "I told you he liked you and not Carmela."

"Can you blame me for the assumption?" I took a quick sip from my cycling water bottle. "Be reasonable, guys go for either Carmela's exotic beauty or your brains. Never my girl-next-door looks. Who wants dishwater blonde with lanky legs when you can have exotic or brainy with breasts? Not that men could have your breasts, but you get it."

"Yes, but which of us married first?" Tracy paused. "I'm sorry."

I shrugged. My hand clutched two wedding rings suspended from a gold chain around my neck. Like always, their presence gave me comfort. Tracy poked me.

"I wanted to do mountain biking instead of road cycling," she said. "But no, you desired a five day road ride across Colorado. It'll be fun, you said, something different. From now on I'll land in dirt and mud, not on asphalt, thank you very little." Tracy couldn't retain a straight face.

Her look made me chuckle. The release of tension in my shoulders felt good. I tried to ignore the knots in my legs from not stretching after the forty-five mile ride. We missed the last eleven, because of the accident. Tomorrow we'd face more, if we continued.

Metal curtain rings squealed as the Irishman revealed his friend, resting in the bed beside Carmela's. The new man could have been Christopher Reeve's nephew or at least a shoe-in for Clark Kent. No wonder Carmela struck up a conversation on the ride.

"Is she okay?" His splinted leg—supported on pillows—couldn't maneuver well.

"She's fine." Tracy navigated to the other side of Carmela's bed. She sat at the foot, hissing at the pain in her leg. I hurried to

An Accidental Meeting

help, but she waved me off. "I'm Tracy and this is Carmela, but you know that already from me shouting her name. Sorry for the girlish hysterics on the mountainside. I'm usually better poised. Or at least that's what my girlfriend tells me."

The man in blue blinked as if he didn't catch Tracy's hint. I crossed my arms and tried not to comment something sarcastic. Tracy smiled.

"And this brooding wench with the elf-like reflexes is our dear friend, Teagan."

"I'm Francis Jacobson," the blue-eyed man said. "If you need advice or directions we live nearby."

"Us, too," Tracy said. Francis looked disappointed.

The Irishman studied me. I flushed.

"I don't have pointy ears," I said. "Just a normal woman. Sorry to disappoint."

"In that, you're wrong," the Irishman said. "Elf-like is an apt phrase. Your agility allowed you to escape an accident which knocked out eight people surrounding you."

"I followed you instead of my friends. You saved me. Thank you ... I don't even know your name," I said. With no pockets I didn't know what to do with my hands. I settled for running them through my bobbed hair, then regretted it when he held out his hand to shake mine.

"Jimmy Patrick, from County Cork, Ireland." His grip felt warm and strong, but his smile remained gentle. "Pleased to meet you, Little Poet."

"Excuse me?" I said.

"Your name means little poet in Gaelic, don't you know?" The green of the man's eyes shimmered, as if lit from within by a secret fire: "Do witty words and good deeds stalk your every move, Teagan? Or do adventures follow in your wake?"

I was saved the need to answer when a ride official joined us carrying a clipboard. A logo-emblazoned T-shirt wrinkled over his button-down Oxford. Black-framed glasses edged down his nose. He shoved them upwards.

"The van will leave for the campsite in ten minutes out front. We cannot wait longer. Anyone who doesn't sleep at Base Camp won't start tomorrow morning. Will any of you drop out due to injuries?"

"I–" I began, but Tracy smacked my arm.

"Teagan will ride on. The two of us will not." Tracy gestured at the unconscious Carmela. "Give me your clipboard and I'll write our names down."

He did so. I fought the urge to write my own name. I needed privacy to discuss this with Tracy, but hospitals and privacy mix worse than popcorn and Gummy Bears.

"Count me out. Broken arm I could ride with, but not this break." Francis indicated his splinted lower leg. The man took down names from others nearby then left.

I argued quietly with Tracy about why I should stay until my voice rose into that squeaky realm I detested. We both stopped when a quiet voice interrupted us.

"Can I have some water?" Carmela said.

"Bless you, girl." Tracy grabbed Carmela's hand. "You scared us."

"What are you arguing about?"

"Tracy says I must ride on, but I should stay. Help you." I thrust a cup to Carmela's lips, but she pushed it away.

"We're doing this ride to revive the Teagan we love. If you stop we won't accomplish our goal. Please, you must –" Carmela pushed up, but a wave of dizziness hit her.

I placed my hand on her shoulder. She waved me away and clutched her head. "I'm fine, but you aren't yet. You must get back in the saddle and riding again. I'm sorry we had an accident to bring up old memories, but I'm fine. Really, I am. Don't look at me like that."

An Accidental Meeting

Her words sent a wave of grief across my face. My husband supported my desire to do more than ride a century. But his support became our downfall. A wave of emotion shook me.

"I detest hospitals." Tears clouded my vision, giving the ER lighting a glow. "I need air."

I scrubbed tears off my cheek as I shoved the exit door open. Sunlight blinded me. I tried to gather in the warmth to push aside the chill in my soul and my skin, but sorrow clouded my thoughts. Clouds reflected off the windows along with the sun. Two nurses in scrubs hurried past swinging their lunch bags. I followed the path they abandoned.

Hearing the gentle splash of a fountain, I stumbled toward the sound.

My shoes crunched on gravel. A tiny fountain with a half-circle bench seat hid in a rosemary-scented alcove. I sought shelter there from the storm in my heart. The stone seat cooled my aching legs. I shivered. Sorrow became my cloak and rosemary my nursemaid.

Another pair of feet shifted the gravel nearby. I glanced up.

Jimmy held out his neon yellow rain jacket.

"Forgive me for interrupting. You'll be wanting a coat, Teagan, to expel the chill."

I let tears continue their path down my dusty cheeks. Fighting numbness, I thanked him and accepted the windbreaker around my shoulders. His warm hands didn't linger. Instead he sat beside me on the small bench.

His long legs pressed against mine reminded me I wasn't alone in this world. Their strength and warmth overwhelmed me with a deep ache. I longed for my husband beside me in place of this sweet and oddly handsome stranger.

Birds chirruped in the chartreuse leaves above us, transporting the tiny alcove into a haven for nature. I welcomed their chatter.

Barbara Bagwell

"We cannot push the decision to ride on, can we?" I said. "That ride official said ten minutes."

Jimmy nodded. He studied the fountain instead of me.

"Will you be taking the bus then? Or staying with your friends?" Jimmy said.

"Will you?" I wasn't sure why his answer seemed important. I hardly knew the man.

"I'd like nothing more than to continue. I relocated to Denver for work. Next week I will program for…well, that's not important." Jimmy leaned forward to run his fingers through the icy fountain. "Francis is a great friend, but he's my only friend in the States. Taking this ride provided the chance to meet others. I want to finish, but not without someone to share the experience."

Rainbows circled in drops of water off his fingers. My hand gripped the rings nestled against my skin. I let my eyes lose focus and bared my thoughts aloud.

"My husband once promised to share every day with me. We wrote it into our vows." I swallowed back the pain and continued, content to share something personal within this surreal grotto. "He kept his promise . . . up until he suffered from an aneurysm on a bike ride across the Appalachians. A trip I made him ride so I could get stronger and ride longer. He said I didn't need to push myself, but I insisted on a four day ride. One minute he rode up a shady lane beside me and the next moment he collapsed. I reached his side too late."

Jimmy's fingers withdrew from the water. He ran both hands through his hair and leaned on his knees. He seemed to struggle with something.

"Did I share too much?" I said. "I'm sorry. I'm an open book. Have been for two years."

"That's a long time to be alone. You deserve better." Jimmy's eyes rose to mine.

"We cannot always keep the promises we make, can we?"

An Accidental Meeting

"Promises are just words. It's trusting the other will be there until they can no longer do so that's the hard part. It seems your husband did that."

"Trust has never been my trouble. I just . . . I cannot handle the pain of loving again."

"But you kept loving Carmela. Though—God forbid—she could have been separated from you. I honor you with deep respect for your devotion to a friend."

"You speak differently than most." I smiled at his words. "Is that part of being an Irishman or are you employing Irish blarney on me?"

"Ah, the wench has dimples. Why ever do you hide such scrumptious treats?"

I grinned at his words, not caring about my dimples or the laugh lines around my eyes.

"I promise I won't hide them from you." I offered my hand.

Instead of the quick handshake I expected, Jimmy gripped it a little too long.

"Fair enough, will you also trust I will cycle with you—as long as I am able—for the rest of this ride? I could use a friend."

"Me, too . . . Let me tell the girls I'm moving on."

The orderly took Carmela away in a wheelchair to be admitted. Tracy promised to update me. I hugged and wished them well. It wasn't until I reached the van that I realized my last water bottle rested in the curtained ER room.

"I forgot something," I told the van driver. I hurried—as much as clip shoes will let you run—into the ER. This time the smells and sounds of pain did not toss me into a wallowing despair. I felt hope for the first time in years. I could make it through the day.

Uncertain Promise

My water bottle rested right where I left it on the guest chair. I took a long gulp. Voices filtered through the now-closed curtains. I must admit: I eavesdropped.

"Maybe I should stay here, Francis?" Jimmy said.

"You stay and I call you a coward. You need this as much as she does from what you described. It's been five years since you lost Elise. Teagan doesn't look a thing like her. Don't glare at me. It's a good thing she's different. It won't make you remember how Elise slit her own wrists in a bathtub the night she married you."

A shaky hand rose to cover my mouth. Tears invaded my eyes.

"Is it necessary to speak the words aloud saying my wife committed suicide on our wedding night? That's supposed to be the happiest day . . . How can I trust anyone after such betrayal?"

"Keeping the words in your heart won't make them go away. It's still a fact."

"Francis, if you weren't my friend– "

"Cut yourself some slack, man. You didn't cause Elise's depression. You sheltered her from it. This new girl isn't depressed; just recovering from grief. Like you. Give her a chance."

"Alright, I will. Even if Teagan becomes a friend and no more I will consider it a success. I want to know her better. Behind her troubled eyes a gentle spirit and loving soul hides."

"Life is the journey, my friend, not the destination. Go live it."

A thud-thud of back slapping echoed through the curtain at me. When a male orderly arrived to change Carmela's bed sheets, I walked away.

"Teagan? Are you with me?" Jimmy said behind me. I gave a timid smile and turned.

"I'm with you. Let's finish this adventure."

"Finish? No, my dear, let's start life's next adventure."

I smiled and didn't hide my joy.

Nidhi Khosla *is a freelance writer, food enthusiast, traveler and Assistant Professor at the University of Missouri-Columbia. "Begin Anew" is her first full-length story. In 2013, her piece, "The Homecoming" received an honorable mention in the Daniel Boone Regional Library's flash fiction contest in Columbia, Missouri. Her flash fiction is currently featured in* Interpretations II, *an exhibition of visual and literary art at the Columbia Art League in Columbia, Missouri. Born and raised in India, she aspires to write about immigrants' experiences in the West.*

Nidhi came to the United States in 2005 on a student scholarship. She earned a Master in Public Health degree from the University of North Carolina at Chapel Hill and a PhD in Public Health from the Johns Hopkins Bloomberg School of Public Health. She has published three short reflection/satirical pieces in national newspapers in India , The Indian Express *and* Hindustan Times.

Begin Anew

Nidhi Khosla

Fiction

Nancy Dar finished pinning the *pallu* (end) of her gorgeous Kashmiri silk sari. The sari was covered with beautiful pink and green paisleys, flecked with yellow dots that almost looked golden. She lifted the sari above her ankles to keep from tripping as she walked down the steps of her red-brick house. Nancy was a Resident physician at a community hospital and had moved to the Midwest a year ago. She had fallen in love with the house and purchased it. She had reasoned that the thrill of owning a house would soon wear off. However, a year later her love still held strong. "Just like my feelings for Stanley," she thought happily.

Clutching the pleats of her sari, she got into her shiny new BMW to drive to a party at an Indian family's home seventy-five miles away. The hosts learned that she too was Indian, single and lived alone, and they reached out to her. "Come, meet some *apne log* (own people)," they had said. It was a welcome invitation. This winter had been particularly brutal with leaden gray days, heavy snow and ice. The last few days, she had stayed home indoors after work, imprisoned by the unforgiving cold and icy sidewalks. A vague sense of dread had begun to fill her. She did not know why.

The dinner would be a nice opportunity to relax, she thought. It might be somewhat mundane. At the same time, it would be satisfying to see Indian faces, hear familiar phrases in Indian accents and savor Indian food. Indian cuisine actually comprised distinct sub-cuisines. The cuisine of her native state, Kashmir was subtle yet rich. Sadly, outside Kashmiri circles, one never encountered the traditional delicacies such as *gushtaba*, velvety-soft minced mutton meatballs, or *yakhni*, a fragrant gravy with myriad sweet spices including fennel, cinnamon and cardamom. She missed Kashmiri food. Still, Indian food, the potpourri of different sub-cuisines ruled by butter chicken, was a relief in a foreign land where "spicy" was mistakenly equated with "chiles" or "hot."

After Nancy carefully merged on to the interstate, she began to relax. An Indian couple sped past her. "You can fly on the interstates in the U.S.," she said wryly to herself. Indian highways in contrast could be very bumpy. Several years ago, a trip in India involving an hour-long drive on the highway had left her with a crick in her neck that lasted three days.

Looking at the snow piled in the interstate median, she remembered that she needed to buy a bigger shovel. "I need a man to do manly jobs," she said to herself. After a few minutes, she thought about calling Stanley, her boyfriend, but decided against it. It would be three o'clock in the morning in India, too early to call. Stanley was a white, American man who surprisingly lived contentedly in a small town in India. Stanley had contacted her through an Indian matrimonial website. These websites were similar to Western dating websites but designed with a culturally-appropriate emphasis on marriage instead of dating.

Begin Anew

Indians were obsessed with weddings, which were a family affair. Indian matrimonial profiles often included details of the relatives (all well placed), property ownership and time and place of birth of the future bride or groom (to match horoscopes). She had read several profiles that said that the boy's mother was "a pious, religious lady." Nancy giggled as she imagined a cartoon of the map of India, populated with faceless, pious women, their heads covered with their sari pallus.

Westerners on the other hand were obsessed with sex. Their dating profiles asked questions such as "Would you have sex on the first date?" The question itself would shock most Indians.

Stanley's profile was decently written, though some details were incorrect as she later learned. He had floored her with his knowledge of India, canny insights and gentlemanly Midwestern manners. On their first date, he told her that he moved to India for career growth and had been living there for twenty years. "Now, I might move, especially if my future wife wants to live elsewhere," he grinned. Nancy's ears pricked up at the mention of the word 'wife.'

"So he won't waste my time," she thought, unlike several crazies she had met who were looking for "friends" in a matrimonial website. She had quickly shifted her attention back to what he was saying, chiding herself silently to take things easy.

He told her that he had met some Indian girls. The Indian girl he had met before meeting Nancy, was a Christian. They had chatted for three months. The girl's parents wanted him to give his decision but he wanted more time. He called it off. The girl had been genuinely hurt, "but what can I do?" he said.

"But you knew, didn't you, that in arranged marriages, one is expected to decide after a few meetings at the most?" Nancy remarked. He did not reply.

Stanley and Nancy maintained their long-distance relationship. Their phone and Skype calls followed a comfortable routine, with the occasional surprise call which gave her much joy. He would tell her how his week went. She would share her news. He would laugh at her stories. Life was sweet and fulfilling. She was fortunate to get a well-read, kind and shy man. An Indophile American who respected her and her culture, had never tried to act fresh, but instead was the soul of courtesy, was a rare find.

She turned off the interstate and arrived at her hosts' house. The house was tastefully decorated. Brightly painted, hand-made figurines from different Indian states lent an eclectic touch to the western decor. There were about fifteen guests including four older couples in their 60s. "*Namaste* Aunty, *Namaste* Uncle", she greeted the couples after her hosts introduced her to them. In several South Asian countries, older people are often respectfully addressed as "Uncle" and "Aunty" even if they are complete strangers. They were surprised that she could speak Hindi and even more surprised when they learned she was Indian. She had encountered such reactions even earlier. Her Hindu parents had chosen to name her Nancy, a distinctly non-Hindu name. A lifetime of confusion ensued because hardly anyone believed that someone named Nancy could be Hindu. Having a rare last name did not help either. The billion plus Indians had relatively few Dars, easy to miss. Her fair skin further confused people.

An uncle said, "Oh, come on. We are all Indians only. You can tell us your real name!" Nancy responded politely that it was her real name.

Dinner was served. There was *paneer* (homemade cheese) curry, *daal makhani* (lentils with cream), butter chicken, several vegetarian curries brought by the guests and *naan* (a leavened white flatbread). *Naan* is ever-present at Indian gatherings in America. Nancy was amused when her non-Indian friends once said they thought Indians must make *naan* daily at home.

"What *naan*-sense!" Nancy quipped, her eyes twinkling. "Actually, most Indian kitchens don't have ovens. We eat *naans* only

Begin Anew

at parties or at restaurants."

The hostess had prepared *gajar-ka-halwa*, a winter specialty made with grated carrots, slow cooked with *ghee*, sugar and milk, till the milk evaporated. It was flavored with powdered green and black cardamom, and garnished with slivered almonds and cashews.

Nancy filled her plate with the home-cooked dishes aunties had brought, avoiding the chicken, *dal makhani* and *naan* that had been catered.

The dinner conversation revolved around careers and marriages of the family members of the guests. "Marriage only happens at 'the right time,'" said an aunty with a wave of her hands. The others nodded in agreement. Nancy wondered how one knows if it is the "right time" or the "right person." She had a good job, a nice boyfriend, a lovely house and a fancy car. It was a joy to reflect on how the details were falling into place. She had been invited to Stanley's parents' house and had met them a few times subsequently. So the important American ritual of "Meet the Parents" had been done. He joked that his Indian colleagues teased him continuously about getting married. The teasing increased after they learned about Nancy.

Stanley had met her parents as well. Her parents did not feel comfortable around him. "He won't care about you when he has work. You were standing there with a glass of water. He did not bother to look up," her mother had said. Other family members said he was not affectionate. Nancy did not know what to make of these reactions. Maybe deep down her family was prejudiced towards a non-Indian, non-Hindu and were trying to find an excuse to dissuade her. They theoretically liked foreigners, but might balk at a foreign prospective son-in-law.

"The most important thing is that he is really kind-hearted," Nancy had said repeatedly. But her family was not convinced.

The host came over to ask Nancy how she was doing. "I am

fine," Nancy said extra-brightly, embarrassed that she was lost in her thoughts.

Nancy followed the host to the kitchen and offered to help him heat the *gajar-ka-halwa*. The kitchen reminded her of her close friend Jon's kitchen. She had wanted to tell Jon about Stanley but hesitated. "How does one tell about your significant other who has not been declared to be such?" she pondered. When she finally, tentatively, asked Stanley what their relationship was, he laughingly confirmed that she was his girlfriend. *Voila!* It was so simple. She had needlessly complicated it in her mind, wondering what his intentions were and worrying how it would work out. He had told her when they first met, that distance would not be a problem. "I will work out something," he had said. But she had secretly doubted the possibility, until then.

"Girlfriend, girlfriend," she had repeated to herself then. It sounded good. She felt like Toni Collete's character Rose in the 2005 movie, *In Her Shoes*. In the movie, when Rose, a sincere, career-minded woman finally finds love, she says she is going to repeatedly say the word "boyfriend" because she never really had one before. It was the same for Nancy.

Nancy, now officially a girlfriend, had started to tell close friends about Stanley. It made a nice story, Indian girl in U.S. meets American guy living in India. Her friends were supportive, though puzzled because American men were typically more forward than Stanley. She was, however, content. "It is like a demure 1960s *Bollywood* romance, but in the Internet age" she explained to Jon who gaped incredulously. "Our love is mutually understood. There is no physical display of affection, just as in those movies."

She wondered what her neighbors would think when Stanley would visit her. Her neighborhood comprised mostly Midwestern, white folk. They were welcoming and helpful. She sensed they were still trying to figure out "the Indian girl." She paid the son of a neighborhood family to mow her lawn during the warmer months.

Begin Anew

He seemed to mow everyone's lawn. She wanted to show she was one of them by complying with the unspoken neighborhood practice. "Plus who knows, behaving like 'them' might make the neighbors like me more," she thought.

The dessert was ready, and she helped her host serve it.

"So are you renting an apartment, *beti* (daughter)?" asked an uncle kindly.

" No, I own a house," Nancy replied.

Buying a house was an Americanized act for a single Indian girl. Her parents had accepted her expensive car but the house purchase had been dubbed extravagant and unwarranted. After all, girls got married and moved to their husband's house. So what was the need for her to buy a house? But Nancy had held her ground and rationalized that it was better to invest in a mortgage than pay rent.

The dinner ended. Guests started to leave. Nancy said her goodbyes as well. She returned home and called Stanley, excitedly telling him about the party. He did not respond cheerfully. She had an intuition that something was wrong.

Next day, Nancy was not feeling well. She called Stanley again and said, "I am not well." She started crying. He listened silently for a minute, told her to take some rest and hung up.

Hurt, Nancy decided she was not going to call until he did. He called after an agonizing week. She told him, "I am still unwell. I would like it if you would call to check on me when you know I am unwell."

He said nothing. She fought to stem the rising panic. They exchanged some perfunctory comments and hung up. He did not call during the week to check on her.

A week later, he called on Skype but kept his camera switched off. "I just want to be upfront. Right now we are just friends. I don't know how much time I need, to know if we have chemistry," he said.

Nancy clutched at her desk for support. The world seemed to spin a little faster.

"I thought we had chemistry," she mustered. Silence.

"All I know is that I care very deeply for you." Silence.

"I don't want to pressure you but if I am nowhere on your priority list, please tell me frankly," she sobbed. Even in her despair she was concerned that he should not feel guilty.

He finally spoke again, "There is no one else." It did not console her.

"We need to talk more. When we speak next time, please keep your camera on," she said. She drank water, breathed deeply and suddenly laughed, "You know I can survive anything, don't worry about me." They hung up. She shook her head at her emotional reaction. Everything would be alright. He is a kind person. He must be having a bad day.

Five days later, he sent her an email breaking off the relationship. It said nothing about whether he had ever cared for her. There was no apology. Instead it said, ". . . enjoyed getting to know you a little," and he wished her the best. The email was written in two different font types which suggested it had been edited. How heartless! He had sent it cold-bloodedly, without sparing a thought for her feelings.

Nancy fought back her tears. She had a full day ahead at the hospital. She would cry later. At night, she started to discard the few things she possessed that had a connection with him. There were no love letters to be burnt. "Emails can't be destroyed," she laughed hysterically. They exist unseen in virtual reality even when deleted. There were receipts of some sightseeing, ice-cream, a frayed wristband she had worn daily and two old idols of Hindu gods that he had gifted to her. Had he forgotten that he had actually told her earlier that he needed to get rid of the old "junk"? She felt pained once again that he had chosen to give a used, cheap item as a gift.

Begin Anew

She started to browse Kashmiri recipes on her iPad. She rarely cooked, but reading traditional recipes comforted her. The mind however is rarely content in focusing on the present. Her thoughts strayed again to wondering "why?" She remembered her mother's admonishment about him. She recalled he had broken off contact with the other girl under a similar pretext. A leopard does not change its spots.

She went to bed and eventually sleep overpowered her.

Next day, Nancy had her hair styled. It was time to get back to dating again. "You look nice. What's the occasion?" a colleague asked. Nancy just smiled.

Over the next few weeks, she made herself busier with work. Work was a better healer than time, she thought. Tears would sometimes well up in her eyes, surprising her because she thought she was over the break-up. One often pulls off a scab prematurely, expecting the wound underneath has healed but the wound is still raw. She was impatient to move on. She was dismissive of the severity of the wound caused by the broken relationship. After all, the guy had implied that the relationship itself had never existed.

One afternoon she was consulting the hospital chaplain concerning a difficult case of a patient who was refusing to acknowledge his fatal diagnosis. The chaplain said, "A wound that is unwept and unmourned does not heal." Nancy nodded and continued discussing the case.

At night, her thoughts drifted to the chaplain's words. Indians do not mourn losses other than death. Even India's ghastly 1947 Partition had not been mourned or remembered through memorials. Americans in contrast, create a memorial for everything. Stoicism ran in her blood. She had not mentioned to anyone about the break-up. Next day she related how he had abruptly ended things, to her colleague who knew a little about her relationship with Stanley. The colleague was supportive. Encouraged, Nancy slowly confided to a few close friends as well. It started to hurt less. The chaplain had been right.

She started to go out more as the weather started to mellow. Spring was coming. Trees had little raised nubs that would soon become buds and then flowers.

It was Friday. Nancy was driving to attend a traditional wedding shower hosted by the same Indian family that she had visited two months ago. The interstate extended before her. Grass shone emerald green in the medians and beyond the shoulder. The sky was mostly clear with some friendly clouds. The afternoon sun's rays were diaphanous silver grey arrows, peeking out from under the clouds. As the road undulated up and down, she could see in the rearview mirror the trail of traffic behind her. New cars met her along the way and separated off the exits, like new friends you meet and spend time with before life takes them their separate way. The world seemed to beckon and life was full of hope and surprises waiting to be discovered. She was beginning anew.

Theresa Elders *Terri's first byline appeared in 1946 on a piece about how bats saved her family's home from fire, published on the children's page of the* Portland Oregonian. *At nine years old, she hadn't known "Bats in Our Belfry," would lead readers to suspect her family's sanity. Unrepentant, she's continued to spill the beans, sharing secrets in the form of anthology stories. Her indiscretions have been featured in a hundred books, including* Chicken Soup for the Soul, A Cup of Comfort, Thin Threads, *and* HCI Ultimate. *A licensed clinical social worker, in 2003 UCLA's School of Public Policy and Social Affairs honored Terri as a Distinguished Alumna. In 2006 she received the UCLA Alumni Award for Community Service. Terri has edited several books for Publishing Syndicate, and is delighted to be a "co-creator" for the* Not Your Mother's Book *series. She blogs at http://atouchoftarragon.blogspot.com.*

Blame and Shame

Theresa Elder

Creative Nonfiction

I'm no saint, but I've led an upstanding life. I've been a high school teacher, a psychiatric social worker, a Peace Corps Volunteer, a wife (twice) and a mother (once). I've worked for federal, state and municipal governments and as a local contractor for three years for a foreign republic. Even in retirement, I serve on boards, councils and commissions. You'd probably regard me as a pillar of the community, a poster child for civil behavior.

You'd never suspect that I'm a criminal who spent a night behind bars.

When newscasts feature police wrestling along suspects in what's become known as "the perp walk," I start to shiver. Been there, done that, I think, rubbing my forearms to beat down the persistent goose bumps. Time does not heal all wounds. I know. It's been over fifty years since I found my law-abiding self literally crossing the line, yet I still shudder when I think about getting arrested.

Theresa Elders

That night so many years ago when my husband and I set off for a Christmas party the evening before Christmas Eve—which we jokingly alluded to as Christmas Eve-Eve—we looked forward to downing a few screwdrivers, trading tall tales with Bob's fellow police officers, and ending our holiday revels with a midnight feast of steak and eggs at Hody's Drive-in. That was the pattern we usually followed on our rare nights out.

Bob had worked as a patrolman on what the Long Beach Police Department then called the "early three" shift, 3 p.m. to 11 p.m., for the two and a half years he'd been on the force. With little seniority, he also worked weekends. So on December 23, 1958, we took our ten-month-old son to Bob's parents' home for a sleepover and set off for the party. We weren't whistling Christmas carols, but we certainly felt infused with holiday spirit.

"It's not too bad having Tuesdays and Wednesdays off," Bob remarked, maneuvering our old Plymouth into a tight parking space on the palm-tree-lined suburban street. "At least this year we can go to a party, have Christmas Eve lunch with my folks and laze around Christmas morning before I have to go back to work Thursday afternoon."

"True. It worked out pretty good this year," I agreed. "We'll have our Christmas dinner before you leave. The turkey's small enough that I won't have to get up too early Christmas morning to get it in the oven."

Every once in a while we talked about how nice it would be if Bob worked day shifts and enjoyed weekends off, a more traditional lifestyle. I hoped that once our son was in school, Bob could get assigned to days. But privately, I actually enjoyed having him out of the house on weekend afternoons. As soon as he'd leave, I'd plop the baby down for a nap and pick up a book. I was a junior that year, majoring in English at Long Beach State College, carrying some tough literature courses that required a lot of reading and writing. When Bob was home, he'd watch *I Love Lucy* reruns and quiz

Blame and Shame

shows, and in our little two-bedroom house, even in the bedroom with the door closed, I could hear the blare of the television. I longed to set up my portable Smith-Corona on the dining room table, but had to settle for tapping away while sitting cross-legged on the bed.

What a great break for us to have a night out, I thought again, as we entered our host's house. The living room already was packed, so it took us some time to greet friends and weave our way around the Christmas tree to get to the kitchen where Bob set a quart of orange juice and fifth of vodka on the counter. In those "bring your own bottle" days, we always drank screwdrivers. Because I didn't much enjoy the acrid taste of vodka, I always took mine pretty light. But the evening was not far along before I noticed that Bob skimped on the O.J. when he mixed his own drinks.

Clutching our highballs, we returned to the living room. I joined a group of women on a sofa; Bob huddled with some buddies in a corner. In the late '50s, the sexes rarely mingled at cop parties. The guys talked shop and exchanged risqué jokes. The gals discussed babies and recipes for clam dip or pecan sandies. In those days, few policemen's wives worked. The men still believed it a disgrace to their manhood if they weren't singlehandedly supporting their family.

When Bob shared the news that I intended to become a high school English teacher, his friends would shake their heads. "I'd never let my wife work," they would say. "It's terrible for the kids."

"Well, my mom worked. She and Dad were both nurses, and I grew up all right," my husband would reply.

I wasn't surprised that evening that none of the women I sat with showed much interest in what I was reading in my literature courses, even though one or two did ask about my classes. I listened to the chatter about teething remedies and diaper rash, nodded and smiled, and every once in a while, bored to bits, wandered into the kitchen to replenish my drink.

Not long before midnight, Bob sidled over and jerked his head towards the bedroom where I'd stashed my purse and jacket.

"Let's head on out," he said. "Doc thinks it would be fun to drive down to Orange County to grab some breakfast at an all-night diner he likes down near Newport."

I hesitated. I could tell by the slight glaze in his eyes that Bob had put a big dent in the fifth of vodka.

"Do you think it's safe to leave Long Beach?"

Bob had told me more than one story about Long Beach police being pulled over by fellow officers and kicked loose as a courtesy. It seemed to be an unspoken code that a cop didn't write a DUI for a fellow cop.

"Sometimes we make a guy park his car and we'll give him a lift home. But we don't arrest each other," he'd explained.

"Hey, it's only about an hour away. I'm fine."

Then Doc approached. A burly man, probably a decade older than most of the officers there that night, Doc had a reputation for heavy boozing and womanizing. He was one of the few officers attending who'd not brought along his wife. Bob had mentioned earlier that Doc's wife didn't like parties. That never seemed to stop Doc from attending, and he'd usually be the only man in the room chatting with other men's wives, and flirtatiously, too.

"Let's go," he caroled. "I'm feeling full of the Christmas spirit tonight. Breakfast will be on me."

Bob winked at me. We'd had barely enough left after buying our Christmas turkey to cover the cost of steak and eggs at Hody's. Doc's offer to pick up the tab at a café likely to be more costly than our neighborhood drive-in was a real bonus for us.

So we took off, Bob behind the wheel, Doc in the passenger seat, and me tucked into the cramped back seat of the old Plymouth. As we headed south, I began to get drowsy. Apparently, I drifted off to sleep because the next thing I knew I could hear Bob arguing with somebody who didn't sound like Doc.

Blame and Shame

I opened my eyes and jerked my head around to check my surroundings. We'd pulled into a service station.

"Bob's drunker than I thought," Doc whispered. "I noticed he was weaving when he went in to pay the attendant for the gas."

The service station attendant approached the car.

"I think this guy has had too much to drink," he said. "Can anybody else here take the wheel?"

I blinked and shook my head. I still hadn't mastered a stick shift, didn't even have a driver's license.

"There's no problem," Bob insisted. "I can drive."

When Doc remained quiet, I realized he probably was drunk as well. I thought I'd heard a slight slur when he remarked about watching Bob walk.

The attendant grimaced and headed back to the station. We took off.

About five minutes later, as we neared the outskirts of Newport, I heard the wail of a siren and swiveled my head around to face flashing lights.

Bob pulled the Plymouth to the side of the road. He and Doc traded stricken glances.

A pair of Orange County sheriffs approached and Bob rolled down his window.

"A service station attendant phoned and described a 1949 blue Plymouth. He said he thought the driver was intoxicated. We're going to have to ask all of you to take some tests."

I was sober enough to realize I'd be asked to walk a straight line and perform other balancing tricks, like a trained seal. Edging out of the car, I realized that my boredom earlier in the evening had led me to the kitchen counter more times than I'd actually counted. I wasn't drunk, but I certainly was intoxicated. I began to explain as much to the sheriff.

"I don't know how to drive a stick shift," I began, "Or I'd have taken the wheel."

Uncertain Promise

Bob and Doc stared at me and shook their heads. I shut up.

I managed to walk heel-to-toe without wavering, but when I had to put my arms straight out and balance on my left foot, I swayed. My right foot thumped down before I toppled over. I'd flunked the test.

The three of us were booked at the Orange County jail. They charged Bob with driving under the influence, Doc and me with "intoxicated in auto." I was herded into a tiny, solitary cell.

"Great," I thought. "Now what? Will the guys lose their jobs? What about me? Will I ever get a school district to hire me now, with an arrest record?"

I curled up on my cot and fell asleep, waking often through the night to agonize over yet another issue. What would Bob's parents think if we didn't turn up by noon to pick up the baby? How would we afford to pay the fine? How would we make mortgage payments if Bob lost his job?

As morning came on, I glanced at the little Elgin watch my parents had given me for my high school graduation. It was nearly eight. I was hungry. I remembered that we'd been drinking on empty stomachs. No need for dinner, we thought, since we'd been saving our appetites for that midnight breakfast at Hody's.

A matron unlocked the door of my cell.

"Come along. Your husband and his friend are waiting for you in the lobby. You can wait there with them."

Bob and Doc glanced at me sheepishly. I realized I must have looked disgusted with them both.

"The bail bondsman will be here in a few minutes," Bob said. "We'll drop Doc off to pick up his car, and head for Downey to pick up the baby."

"We have to stop by the house first. Your parents will know something's wrong if we show up looking all wrinkled and disheveled, as if we'd slept in our clothes. Which we have."

That morning, I got a quick shower and fresh clothes. But I

Blame and Shame

couldn't wash away the overwhelming sense of dread that stayed with me as we struggled through the next few dismal days.

On Christmas morning I went through the motions of fixing a turkey dinner, but neither of us took much pleasure in eating it. That was the first time I'd ever seen my husband turn down seconds on candied sweet potatoes.

Bob and Doc hired a criminal defense attorney friendly to cops, a man known as The Silver Fox. He thought he could plea bargain and get Bob's charge reduced to reckless driving if Doc and I both pled "no contest" to our charges.

"Just what is 'intoxicated in auto' and why is that a crime?" I'd asked.

The lawyer explained that in California public intoxication included passengers over the legal limit in any vehicle that is stopped for any reason.

"For instance," he told us, "if you'd called a cab and the driver blew a red light, you could be arrested for public intoxication."

All I knew was that it sounded unfair. I'd been asleep in the back seat of a car that I didn't even know how to drive.

The ploy worked, though, and Bob kept his job.

Nonetheless, it was only the beginning of a series of humiliating incidents for me. For decades, every time I filled out a job application, I had to explain that, yes, I'd been arrested for a misdemeanor—and I would have to provide the lurid details.

In interviews, I'd find myself blushing as I explained how I got arrested after falling asleep in the back seat of a car after a Christmas party. Most employers were sympathetic, more so than what I'd expect them to be today, when laws are much more stringent about blood alcohol levels and what constitutes intoxication.

The chief damage, though, was to my marriage. I'd lost faith in Bob's ability to exercise good judgment. I blamed him for the whole thing. I never accepted any responsibility in what happened that long ago holiday season. Instead, for years, I just seethed.

Bob's drinking gradually spiraled out of control; he was hospitalized twice with acute pancreatitis as a result. Eventually, he entered an in-patient program, and remained sober for 22 years before he died of unrelated causes.

After twenty-five years of marriage, we divorced.

Years later, filling out an application for the Peace Corps, I got to wondering. I called Bob and asked if that misdemeanor was still on my record in California. I knew he could run a check. When he phoned back, he was chuckling.

"I checked, and there's nothing. It's not there. I'm not certain it's ever been there. They may never have put it on your record in the first place."

All that agony for nothing, I thought, remembering my embarrassment and anxiety every time I switched jobs. All that blame and shame…for nothing. All that hostility and rage…for nothing.

Even so, I answered truthfully on the Peace Corps application. Yes, I'd been arrested. It really happened, whether it had been recorded or not. The Peace Corps has the FBI do background checks on applicants. I certainly didn't want the FBI to say I'd lied. Besides, there might be some trace that Bob had overlooked.

The truth is…I have been busted.

Only now do I realize that I could have talked Bob out of driving to Newport that long ago December night, pleading a headache or a queasy tummy. I could have maneuvered him away from Doc with promises of late night kisses and cuddles. But I didn't. Knowing it was unsafe, I let him drive.

Instead, I went along willingly. And somebody could have been killed. That night could have ended in tragedy, an outcome far more serious than my chagrin.

I'd been an accomplice. That's my real crime.

Elaine Stewart *is a graduate of the University of Illinois in Champaign-Urbana with a B.S. in Advertising. She has worked a variety of jobs including news editing and public relations and is currently employed at the Columbia Public Library. Her short fiction has appeared in* Well Versed, The Daily Illini *and the* Liberty Bee-Times *and has placed in contests through* Bylines *magazine and the Leah Trelease Prize for fiction. She has completed three novels, one of which was based on her experiences at Midway Atoll in the Pacific, where she lived for several years. She currently writes a blog, Baby Dancer (elainestew.wordpress.com), about her new passion, competitive pro-am ballroom dancing.*

A Young Woman Of Promise

Elaine Stewart

Fiction

Lettie had been trying to reach her ex-husband for a full day before she finally got a call back from him on his cell. She was trying to make arrangements to get the last of her boxes he had been hauling around in the back of his pickup for several weeks. He had been nagging at her to get them, saying he wanted to be done with this final bit of post-divorce logistics, so she was puzzled to find him upset, as if she were pestering him, when she asked where he'd been.

"I'm in Springfield for training," he said. "The boxes aren't with me anyway. They're out at the house."

She hesitated, confused. "Out at the orchard?"

"No, Let. We sold that, remember? They're at my place. I stuck 'em in the garage before I started out yesterday. You can go get them anytime. Angel will let you in."

Still, she had to think a minute before she understood he meant the '60s split level house at the edge of town that had been his Mom's before her death a year before—right before all their trouble began. He had moved into the house after their separation and, in his mind, it had already become 'home.' Even when she finally understood, she stood mute, phone to her ear, taking it in. Had he done this on purpose, wanting her to feel ridiculous, his almost-forty crone of an ex-wife standing on the step asking his young Filipina wife for permission to retrieve her boxes?

Lettie closed her eyes. "She'll need to know I'm coming—" She stopped short when she heard her voice rising, cleared her throat and tried again. "Could you let her know?"

"If you want," he said with a pointedly audible sigh. "When should I tell her you're coming?"

Lettie looked out the window at the bleak spring drizzle. "I heard it may clear off this afternoon. Let's say about one o'clock?"

"Okay, but call her yourself if you have to change that, all right?" He gave her the number at his house. "She won't want to sit around all afternoon waiting."

"Of course." She couldn't help but wonder what the woman would have to do that would make her so impatient. She was virtually certain this new young wife didn't have a job in town yet; Lettie would have heard about it—or seen the woman already at her new post.

Her dog was scratching impatiently to be let out as she clicked off the call. She sighed. "Really, Darcy? We just went out an hour ago." But by now, Lettie knew better than to wait, so she slipped on her rain jacked, clipped the leash to his collar and followed him out, pulling her hood around her face against the wet. A full ten minutes later, they returned to the house where shook out her rain

A Young Woman of Promise

jacket and followed him inside. She dreaded to think how it would be when winter came and the snow was blowing outside instead of rain. After only a couple of weeks, she was finding it difficult to keep up Darcy's routine and had begun eyeing her small savings account, considering paying someone to put up a chain-link fence around the backyard. She knew she should never have gotten a dog when she had no fence, but the dog had been her only consolation after the devastation of her divorce—for which she ultimately blamed herself.

She had known from the beginning, as Thad had not, that theirs was not a soul mate kind of union. He was, in a way, a 'rebound' guy—the one she had turned to, not after being jilted, but in the wake of her public debacle, when she had found herself in the national news, making headlines as the university student journalist who had been so duped by a murderer that she had authored an award-winning article focusing on his kindness.

Lettie had been referred to the man by a daycare center—a local father who was caring for his young family of two boys by himself after his Mexican wife left them to return to her family in Guadalajara. Within a month of the interview and her article's appearance in the student news magazine, the wife's body was found in a shallow grave in a wood not far from the home and the man was to be charged with her murder, but before he could be taken into custody, he had shot his boys and himself to death. Shocked, Lettie was sickened that the man to whom she had listened with such sympathy—had even been a bit in love with—had fooled her so outrageously. She had already gone into shutdown mode when the story broke into the national media and sources began citing her article as an ironic commentary on how evil can be hiding in plain sight among us.

Elaine Stewart

She had dropped out of the journalism program a month before graduation, horrified by her connection with the incident. Adrift, unable to face going home, Lettie had lingered in her college town and eventually met Thad, an Ag School grad who was mercifully unaware of what she had done in her short time as a student journalist. Three months later, she accepted his marriage proposal. Though she had never imagined spending her life in a small Missouri town, her disgrace had changed all that. In fact, it was Thad's rural life she wanted, by then—the promise of anonymity, where she could hide away from the world forever. She never fully explained her dropping to Thad, except to say it was due to stress, which was the truth, after all, in its way. Who wouldn't be stressed, feeling herself in some way responsible for the deaths of two innocent children? She thought about the tragedy of those lost lives and the lost promise of her youth everyday, even now.

Despite, or maybe because of, her knowledge that she had never really loved Thad, she mourned the loss of her marriage, feeling guilty over its demise. Though the indignity of being dumped for a young foreign woman he found through the Internet had wounded her pride, she understood why he had done it. Her understanding had transformed into pain and even anger in the last few weeks, however, when she had learned via the small town grapevine that Thad's twenty-one-year-old young bride was already pregnant. And now it seemed she would have to meet Thad's 'Angel' under the pretext of collecting her ragtag belongings.

Lettie spent the rest of the morning preparing for the incoming load of boxes by unpacking the ones that had been sitting in the garage since her move—two of them full of the wedding china that she had carefully newspaper-wrapped before leaving the orchard house. She hadn't cried when she had hurriedly packed the plates

A Young Woman of Promise

and cups and saucers with their tiny lavender-flowered design and didn't expect to cry now. She and Thad so rarely used the dishes, so she had scarcely ever thought of them. But suddenly, she was weeping as she unwrapped each item. The dishes, so fragile and beautiful, representing happy expectation never realized, brought to mind the other thing that had ultimately doomed her marriage: the fact that after four miscarriages, she and Thad had never produced a child. If there was anything she truly had wanted from her marriage, it had been children. With each truncated pregnancy, Lettie's wish had only grown greater, the pain in her heart deeper.

She quickly stashed the china out of sight at the back of one of the lower cabinets, then slit the tape holding the boxes together at their seams, flattening and propping them against the refrigerator. She felt tears on her cheeks again, and peered out the window over the kitchen sink hoping for once that the drizzle would continue, giving her an excuse not to go out and see Thad's new wife today. But then, as if to mock her, the raindrops diminished and the sun began to peek prettily through the clouds.

Lettie sniffed and reached down to pat Darcy who had come up to lean silently against her side. She could still put off this encounter, she knew, but to do so she would have to call the number Thad had given her and have an awkward phone conversation with the woman, during which her voice might crack or she would break down crying again. No, it was best to get it over with.

She gave Darcy a biscuit and went out to her Civic to let the rear seat down and clear out the trunk. She pulled out her stash of cloth grocery sacks, the large Rubbermaid bin of cleaning supplies she had stowed during the move and the twenty pound bag of winter-emergency kitty litter that never left her trunk. At last she climbed behind the wheel, cast a glance in the rearview mirror to be sure her eyes weren't puffy and then put the key in the ignition.

Elaine Stewart

It was only a five minute drive to where the red-brick split level sat on its tiny lot just beyond the outskirts of town. Thad's parents, both now deceased, had bought the place shortly before Lettie and Thad's wedding; a practical, as well as symbolic gesture of moving out and handing the orchard over to their son. But the place always struck Lettie as impossibly barren compared to the acres and acres of orchard they were giving up. She had expected the couple to landscape their new home, put in at least a few ornamental trees and bushes, annual petunias to brighten the doorstep, but they liked it plain, they said—didn't want green things to bother about anymore. It had seemed to her a lesson in the sad inconstancy of life.

Lettie pulled into the short gravel drive, her heart creeping into her throat as she braked and shut off the engine. The rain clouds had burned away completely and the sun shone full on her face as she stepped from the car, as if onto a hotly-lit stage. She took a deep breath and went to the front stoop where she stood a long, silent moment and then reached out to rap on the door.

There was no sound from inside. The air around her buzzed only with the loud hum of insects—in the grass, she supposed, since there was no foliage. A minute passed with no reply and she knocked again, harder this time. "Hello. Is anyone there? It's Lettie—Lettie Melon. I've come for my boxes. Your, uh...Thad was to supposed to tell you I was coming?"

Lettie put her ear close to the door and that's when she finally heard the other hum—one from some distant corner inside the house. A vacuum. She straightened. Was she really going to have to stand here and wait for who knew how long? Heaving a sigh, she put a hand to the doorknob, twisted and to her surprise found the door gave way easily under hand. She pushed it open and went in.

A Young Woman of Promise

She hadn't been inside the old house for over a year—not since she and Thad had cleared it out after his mother's death—but it still bore the mark of her mother-in-law, with its flowery wallpaper and ruffled curtains. An eerie feeling came over her, in fact, as she stepped into the foyer, as if Thad's mother might appear from the kitchen, wiping her plump hands on a dishtowel.

"Hello?" Lettie called again, but she knew she couldn't be heard. She climbed the short flight of stairs to the upper level from which the whir of the vacuum came. She came to the last bedroom in the hallway and stopped, peering in around the half-closed door. There was the woman, the tiny Filipina, predictably beautiful in a dark, full-faced kind of way, sleek black hair tied back in a long ponytail that flipped behind her as she stood on a chair, moving the vacuum head over the surface of the ceiling fan still an arm's length beyond her reach. The chair was a rickety one Lettie recognized from an old desk set her mother-in-law had kept in her bedroom. One leg had broken off of it at some point. Lettie thought Thad had thrown it away, but here it was, wobbling precariously beneath the weight of the reckless young woman who was working at the fan blades, so determined to expunge grime from the fixture that she had completely thrown aside caution for the fragile new life in her belly.

Lettie watched, transfixed, as if she was being forced to view a cautionary docudrama, destined to offer up a moral she could never forget. Her instinct was to yell at the girl to get down, but she hesitated. What right did she have, how was it even her place, to intervene in this potential tragedy? She shouldn't even be here—and more than that, the girl shouldn't have chosen to get up on a wobbly chair, daring fate to take her and her baby down. Cruel as is seemed, survival of the fittest should still be allowed to shape the species, shouldn't it? But even as this wicked thought wove its way through her head, Lettie was throwing back the bedroom door and striding into the room, hands outstretched, crying out to the girl. "Get down! What are you doing?" She was gathering the small rounded waist in her arms almost before the young woman even registered her presence.

Angel dropped the vacuum and looked at Lettie, giving out a little cry that seemed, oddly, one of both surprise and delight. Still in Lettie's arms, she climbed down from the chair, flicked off the vacuum, and in the sudden silence Lettie's words filled the room.

"Didn't you notice that chair was unstable? You could have fallen and hurt yourself."

But the young woman didn't seem to register the reprimand. She had straightened and was smiling as she studied Lettie's face. "You look like the picture he show me. You his wife, then…" Angel's eyes widened playfully and she laughed out loud. "His wife, I say. Ha! I mean how-you-call…you his ex-wife?"

It would have been offensive, except for the girl's innocence—her obvious amusement at her *faux pas*. Lettie shook her head at first, then nodded. "Yes, I'm Lettie."

"Thad say you come today," Angel said. "I want to meet you before now, but…" She stopped, shrugged. "So, I have cookies. You sit with me and have cookie?"

Lettie shook her head. "I just came to get my boxes. If you can open the garage door, I'll back my car up and load them."

Angel's face fell. "I thought you stay a little bit. Thad is gone. I thought you stay and have cookie with me?"

Lettie stood silent, looking at the young woman. The impish creature was, by almost any standard, just a girl to whom Lettie must seem like a much-missed mother figure. She sighed. "Okay, just for a few minutes. I'd really like to get those boxes home before it starts raining again."

In the kitchen, Angel produced a bag of Oreos, that she placed on the dinette table. She pulled a gallon carton of milk from the refrigerator, found two glasses and filled each one three-quarters full. She continued to watch Lettie closely as they sat munching, and then, finishing her milk quickly, she leaned forward eagerly. "I want you help me."

Lettie blinked, twisting her head uncertainly. "You want my help?"

Angel nodded. "I want to get job."

"You want me to help you find a job?"

"Not find. Just help with this." The girl reached over to the kitchen counter, pulled forth a form and slid it toward Lettie across the table. It was an employment application from the Break Time in town. "I gotta get it right," Angel said. "Spell right and everything and I don't want ask Thad. He busy and..." For the first time Angel's expression showed angst rather than joy. "I don't want him see how I do the words sometimes wrong." She lifted her eyes to Lettie's hopefully.

Lettie stared at the girl, surprised at first, then just puzzled. Was the world this young person grew up in completely devoid of social boundaries, or worse, was Thad making Angel feel so belittled that she was unable to turn to him for help? Or was she just a lonely young woman eager for the company of someone a lot like a mother? Whatever the reason, Angel's round face was filled with expectation, eager.

Lettie looked away, trying for all she was worth to come up with an excuse not to return here to help this young woman. "Okay," she said, finally. "But not today. I'll try to come tomorrow."

"Yes? Okay?" The girl's voice was glad, but still she watched

Lettie, searching her face. "You promise—tomorrow?"

Lettie looked at the girl, then glanced out the window where it seemed the sun would not quit shining now that it had found its way out. She hated it suddenly, even though she had longed for it for weeks now. She lifted her brows, looking the young woman in the eyes. "Yes, tomorrow. I promise."

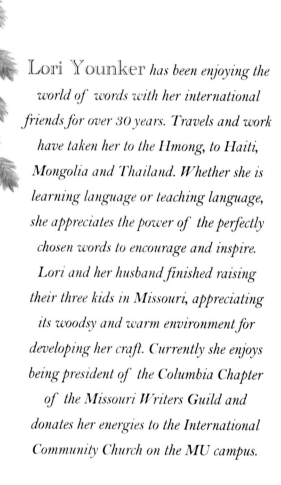

Lori Younker *has been enjoying the world of words with her international friends for over 30 years. Travels and work have taken her to the Hmong, to Haiti, Mongolia and Thailand. Whether she is learning language or teaching language, she appreciates the power of the perfectly chosen words to encourage and inspire. Lori and her husband finished raising their three kids in Missouri, appreciating its woodsy and warm environment for developing her craft. Currently she enjoys being president of the Columbia Chapter of the Missouri Writers Guild and donates her energies to the International Community Church on the MU campus.*

Fahrenheit Meets Celsius

Lori Younker

Creative Nonfiction

The day begins with hot tea, not the thick buttery, salty tea favored by my neighbors, but rather the standard black. I add two spoonfuls of sugar and stir. The tea swirls orange-brown in my mug. I step away from the kitchen to sit on the brightly painted stool next to the wood-stove in the center of our home. I make loud slurping sounds, drawing the tea through my lips. I enjoy my little ritual and decide that I will prefer tea over coffee for the rest of my life.

I think about all the women in shacks and yurts throughout Mongolia who must make keeping warm a priority today. Locally, sources of heat are dwindling; the city's coal bin is nearly empty. Our once formidable stack of kindling outside the front door has been reduced to a humble pile, left-overs from the construction of our "straw bale house" with its eighteen-inch thick bales, covered in plaster, painted white.

I set the mug down on the tile floor to stoke the fire, fighting against the length of the sticks to pack them into the stove. I slam the little black door to push them in as far as they will go. The fire crescendos with a chorus of crackle and hiss. I turn the damper to the left. The clay wall behind the stove is giving off a measure of heat, but even our thick walls are no rival for the January wind that sweeps past the prison, circles the district called "One Well," and beats hard against our edges.

I pick up my tea again and gulp down its hot, sugary goodness; I hope the fire will not go out on my watch. I add a scoop of coal and turn my body to look out the front window that overlooks the yard. Our front window frames our Mongolian horses, a gift to our children to ease the guilt we feel for taking them across the world to live among strangers. The horses stand completely still as they face the rolling hills to the distant west. Their eyes are squeezed shut. I imagine they miss the colors of summer: shades of green, yellow and crystal blue. Their stocky bodies are covered in hoary ice from head to foot with only a circle of color around their nostrils that reveals their coats of black, chestnut, and bay.

"Hang in there, Chocolate," I whisper to the yearling, the youngest of our horses, as if he can hear me. He wears a thick wool blanket, an ineffectual shield from the frigid temperatures. At breakfast, my husband announced to the family that it reached forty-below-zero last night, the place where Celsius and Fahrenheit meet.

"It is the coldest we will see it," he said. "It's awful hard on Chocolate. He should've eaten twice as much as the others this past year, but he wasn't much of an eater."

Before the sun pushed through the clouds, thick from the thousand coal fires that burn around us, my husband Bill delivered the children to school in the company van and went to work. He is the construction manager for an organization that encourages Mongolians on their first try at privately owned business in this

Fahrenheit Meets Celsius

post-soviet, newly capitalistic environment. Thankfully, the engine turned over and they took off for the city. To get it going, Bill placed an electric coil under the oil pan to thin out the sludge until it could circulate freely, like blood through our bodies. Perhaps he kept the coil plugged in the entire night. I try not to pay attention to every detail. The more I know, the more I might be responsible for. Keeping the family fed and encouraged is enough burden for me since I'm not always successful at keeping a stiff upper lip myself.

Before they left, Mary our youngest returned from her outdoor chores and said, "My horse is dying."

"I'm sure he'll be okay," I responded, certain my words would sound empty to an eight-year-old who knows so much more about this country than I.

"We need a vet."

"If it makes you feel better, we'll find one to come out and see him today," I promised. I sent Mary with her siblings, bundled up to her eyes, with her backpack, homework completed, and a little plastic tub of crackers and cheese. She lingered at the fence of the corral and turned around to look at me, only her blonde bangs showing above her sober, green eyes.

Now, an hour later, I wonder how I will find a veterinarian without a phone book, without letting the house get cold. I don't even know how to say "veterinarian" in Mongolian. I get up to thumb through the dictionary.

Thankfully, my language tutor is coming. Her name is Bor, which simply means brown. She will be bundled up in a dark, wool coat that comes to her knees. Beneath her coat will be layers of sweaters and a cashmere vest. Skillfully, she will wrap two scarves around her head and neck until only her eyes are showing. Without these, the cold air on her face would feel like a million tiny knives biting into her flesh. Over several pairs of socks and undergarments, she'll pull on the ever-popular Russian leather boots. Even though they are impractical, she will make the three-mile trek north on their narrow heels. She won't stay home on this frigid day; it's no colder than any other she says, insistent that we meet regularly.

I decide to make her favorite apple cake, the one with chunks of apples and cinnamon. I will insist she take the whole cake to her family. I will fill her bag with mandarin oranges and pay her double for her effort. I imagine her cherry-like cheeks will push her eyes up into half-moons. While putting the cake in the oven, I ponder how little Bor worries about her family, her husband's unemployment, her little refrigerator with its solitary jar of milk.

Our visit starts routinely. She refuses to remove her boots to change into woolen slippers. Perhaps she has considered the ordeal of putting them back on again. In any case, I do not press. She is my elder by at least fifteen years. And she is my teacher, a person of the highest social status here.

As our lesson begins, we both have something on our minds. I need to know how to find a veterinarian. Does she know one? She will think about it and call me later. This is not satisfying, but what can I do? We live in a city without a stable infrastructure. The capital city of Mongolia struggles to keep electricity on for more than five days in a row and to keep its citizens warm. Producing a phone book so a foreigner can find a vet ranks as a very low priority.

But today, my tutor tells me that she is refusing to speak to me anymore. I am shocked. Have I heard her correctly?

"I'm not going to talk to you anymore. Your consonants are so sharp that they hurt my ears, with your t's and k's and g's. Today you will soften everything. You've heard drunken men on the trolleys. Talk like them."

She is serious. She wants me to change the way I speak Mongolian. Right this very minute.

"Read this paragraph, not so ha-toh," she says.

The English equivalent for ha-toh is hard, and it's one of a mere handful of words that sound anything like their English equivalent.

Fahrenheit Meets Celsius

There is the word eet for eat and nudeskin for naked. I would be hard pressed to think of another example.

She drills me on softer articulation, and I promise to remember this new way of speaking at all times. She is pleased and folds her hands and says our lesson is complete. So I serve up hot tea and apple cake, and we stare out the window at the horses. Tsagaa, our sixteen-year-old horse wrangler, has arrived and will take them down for exercise and water. Bor and I watch from the window as he gathers the horses into a herd of four. He opens the gate, but Chocolate will not move. He crumples to the ground, his hind legs failing him. Tsagaa leaves the others and returns to pull at Chocolate's mouth, hoping to put on his harness. The horse clenches his teeth tightly.

Tsagaa enters the house to give me a report, but I know what he will say before he says it. If Chocolate stays on the ground, he will never get back up again.

"Here are five-thousand tugrigs to find a veterinarian for me," I beg, trying to speak with the softness my tutor should appreciate. In my opinion, the Mongolian language sounds like a machine gun with its guttural, monotone delivery. Nevertheless, I strive to produce soft bullets, not hard ones.

"It's too late for a doctor," Tsagaa says wearing black work boots that are too big for him. He stands on the special rug designated for standing and talking indoors with your shoes on. "When I come back from the spring, I will try to work with him. But you could try giving him another bottle of that fennel tea."

He lumbers out the door with the harness still in hand, his sweater and coat too thin, his head uncovered. So, I turn to Bor, "Can you help me feed the horse before you go?"

We brew up the fennel tea, whole handfuls of seeds float to the bottom of the pan, and the water turns a shade of yellow for which there is no name. We try to feed the horse and coax him to open his mouth. He drinks half of a liter and rocks himself back and forth a bit. Even with my ha-toh Mongolian, he will not get up despite all the pulling and coaxing in the world.

My tutor is determined to leave, so I walk her to the bus stop, arm in arm as Mongolians do. I reflect upon this custom. It is more than just enjoying the warmth of another human being. When I'm close to Bor, I am adopted into the Mongol race. Her bloodline flows through me, and I think about how Mongols survive cold winters.

I stoke the fire and make another cup of tea to warm myself. When I try to fill the large kettle for a pot of beef soup, the water comes out of the spigot in slow drips. The car battery that forces water from the tank to the sink is working, but the pipes are frozen.

I will call my husband. There are two major things to worry about, reasons enough to call him away from his work. I will ask him to take the children out of school early. I want them to be here when Chocolate passes away. And the pipes must be thawed before they burst.

The house explodes with excitement at their return. My husband has brought Sukhbaatar with him. He's the oldest in his family, playing the role of father and bread winner for several sisters. His family is forever entwined with ours with a history of holidays spent together, a common employer, and loans. He enters with the others looking eager to be useful.

Pete and Joanna, our older children are convinced they can save the poor horse. They drag out all of their blankets to cover him, and they force the last half of the tea down his throat. Meanwhile, in the water room my husband and Sukhbaatar assesses the condition of our water pipes. This windowless space juts out from the corner of our dwelling, a room designed to store our large tank for water, a castoff from a dairy farm.

My husband finds me and we stand at the window to watch our children's efforts, "Let me eat a sandwich and bring in some more coal and then I'll fetch the vet," he says. "You stay here and

Fahrenheit Meets Celsius

do whatever Sukhbaatar tells you. I think I've found a clinic on the east side of town. Chocolate will make it a few more hours, but we have to take care of the pipes."

I make him a sandwich of summer sausage and sourdough bread. Sukhbaatar has not called for me yet, so I start to chop onions, to peel and dice carrots. I stoke the fire again and return to work peeling potatoes. Sukhbaatar's sister Sara arrives to help me with the noon meal. She cuts and pulls the beef into little chunks and fries them in the wok on the stove. Aromas of meat and onion fill our home.

Now we hear shouts for help from Sukhbaatar in the water closet. He pokes his head out with a terrified look on his face.

"What is it?" I come running.

"Go and get Bill before he leaves. I need him!" his tone is throaty and harsh. I catch Bill going through the gate, and he abandons the vehicle half in the yard and half out. The children follow behind him into the house, all except Mary who has sat down on the frozen ground next to Chocolate, beginning her vigil.

"'Our house in on fire!' Bill is using a voice he has never used before. "Sukhbaatar used a blowtorch to thaw the pipe and a stray piece of straw caught fire. There's fire in the wall. Pete, get an ax and climb on the roof!"

I don't know what to do first. We will need more than water to stop our house from burning to the ground. Joanna, our twelve-year old, has climbed down into the tank of freezing water and is handing up buckets to her father. Her older brother Pete is climbing on the roof with an ax.

"Gouge a hole in the roof!" Bill shouts, but no one hears him except me, so I rush out the front door and shout for Pete to hack through the roof just above where they are working. His first attempts are timid; I am sure his thoughts are on the strangeness of destroying the house he and his father just finished building.

Uncertain Promise

I know we need more help and more buckets, so I cross our yard to the next, forcing Sara to go with me. I have to use my ha-toh voice.

"The big black dog!" she cries.

It's true that the neighbor's dog is a monster, a wolfhound, larger than any other dog in the whole country. But I say, "My house is on fire and you are worried about a dog?"

As we go through the gate in the fence to my neighbor's yard, time slows. I look back to see Sara following on my heels, her face full of fear. I know Mary is with her horse. I know Pete is on the roof. I know Sukhbaatar and Bill are pulling up buckets of water from Joanna who stands knee deep in the tank. I must do something to keep my family in this incredibly challenging country.

I recall our first winter in Mongolia when we lived in a high rise apartment downtown. Even with its semi-modern conveniences there were challenges to survival. I wondered then if I would have the toughness, the resolve to stick it out. Just locating a little meat, a bag of rice, and a head of cabbage could mean hours of hunting through the markets and waiting in long lines. One day in January, a day as cold as this one, I looked out from our sixth floor apartment window at the pastel skies and icy streets. I remembered thinking, "If I don't get out, cold or no cold, and hunt through the market, there will be nothing to eat for dinner."

That strength is still inside me. I march to the neighbors. I am a wild woman who needs their assistance. The next hour is a blur of bodies, a swarm of neighbors, Tsagaa, Sara, Sukhbaatar, me and the children—all struggling to put out the fire. Only Mary is absent. The late afternoon sun throws her shadow across the body of her dying horse.

We save the house. We sit down together in the living room for a plateful of dry noodles tossed with slivers of tasty beef and fried vegetables. When Pete says to pass the ketchup, he looks up at the wide and gaping hole to the cold, dark sky above his bedroom.

Fahrenheit Meets Celsius

The next morning nobody goes to school. I motion for Mary to sit with me by the wood-stove. I will hold back the information I have. Mary can talk circles around us in the local language, find her way through a maze of fenced-in yards, and scare off wild dogs with rocks. As brave as she is, she would not understand that her horse been given away as meat for the poor. Instead, we talk about how sweet Chocolate was, recalling their lovely rides across the open steppes.

"When people die, they lay them out on the top of the mountain for the birds," she says.

"Sukhbaatar will take care of things," I say.

"He was a good horse," Mary says.

"You were a faithful friend, right to the very end," I say, putting a big spoonful of sugar in her tea. I hand her the mug. "I'm so proud of you."

She nods her head and reaches for the tea.

"I'm sorry we couldn't do both," my voice comes in broken pieces. "With everyone helping on the house, there was no one to go and find the vet."

"I know," she says managing a smile.

We huddle together in front of the stove. We are side by side, so close that our arms touch. We each take a sip of our piping hot tea.

C.N. Rowland *is a freelance writer, blogger and poet currently residing in West Fork, Arkansas. She participates in many online and college-based writing groups, as well as poetry readings at The Naked Bean coffee shop. New to the industry, several of her poems:* Summer Come Quick, The Six-Legged Spider *and* You Gently Remind Me *were previously published in the May, 2013 volume of* LSUS Spectra. *Connect with her at C.N.Rowland@aol.com.*

Darwin's Daughter

C.N. Rowland

Creative Nonfiction

"What do you write?" He inquires, with that mellifluous, baritone voice of his. I'm fascinated by the way certain words curl upon his tongue, taking shape with an inflection that is simultaneously different and pleasing.

The room is small and closed in; the only light within falls from the fluorescent bulbs buzzing quietly overhead. The lack of windows makes it feel a little like a tomb to me; a tomb full of tomes. Books paint the walls, pressed and cluttered upon high shelves, and they all tell the story of his vocation. I scan the embossed titles on their spines, but they fail to hook my curiosity to the same degree that he does and so I turn my gaze back to him.

He is seated behind his desk, his elbows propped upon it, supporting the angle of his arms. His hands are fitted together by the graceful lengths of his interlaced fingers, held just below the

Uncertain Promise

curve of his chin. I follow the shape of it up to his mouth, which is courting a small smile. Everything about his body language forms a portrait of comfort, of ease and languor. Beneath the obstacle of the desk, I imagine his legs splayed lazily apart. It occurs to me that, during my regular exposure to him, I have neglected to observe his feet, failed to consider the stance he gains by them and so have nothing to work my imagination around now. I make a mental note to correct this failure later in the week, curtail my annoyance and turn my focus upon his eyes.

If I were forced to pick a favorite feature, it would have to be his eyes, which though dark, flash with warmth, intelligence and mirth. His mouth, so unique in shape that I have never seen its like before, would be a close second, and his effortlessly graceful hands would be third.

Maybe I should feel shame for the directness of my gaze, for the studious way my eyes linger, observe, and catalogue, but I do not. I come to him almost as a child, possessed of equal parts wonder and curiosity; a child trying to sit at a too tall table, staring with wide-eyed fascination over the edge. That's how it feels every time I see him.

What spirit is this that infects me with such wonder? Is it the artist, the writer or the child that finds hidden delight in him? I press around the raw-nerve-interest, suppress and skirt around the embers that waken as if to a sudden draft of fresh air. The stagnation and routine of a quiet life can kill by degrees, and I've been dying for years, a slow death which has made me all the more desperate for meaningful connections, for substance, for growth and expansion, for inspiration, for something worthy of more than momentary fascination—and something in him has acted as an antidote.

I had planned for this meeting the night before, knowing that I would burn quickly through my psychology test and would have some free time before I had to rush off to the tedium of work, to

Darwin's Daughter

my "real" life; time that I could steal for myself, time that I could use to toe my way across the threshold of his office. I knew that I would ace my test, but all the 'A's in the world can't seem to help me understand my own psychological drives, even though there isn't a day that goes by where I don't consider life with a psychologist's eyes.

When I was ten years old, I went with my mother to the local Goodwill store, where we bought all of our clothes and house wares, and where most children would have thrown themselves into the heaps of worn out and over loved stuffed animals and toys, I was busy flipping through the pages of an old college book on psychology. I somehow convinced my mother to buy it and spent many days perusing the information in a haze of confusion and curiosity. For all my love of that science, the art of pinpointing secret motivations in people, I cannot seem to discover even my own purposes. The knowledge gained from my youthful study didn't help me to understand why I was roaming around my house yesterday evening, searching for something—something which would validate my present visit with him. I never did find a valid excuse, but I couldn't shake off the impulse, the need to sit with him, talk to him, listen to him, and study him. So, here I am, using my stolen time to count the buttons on his shirt.

"What do you write?" His query hung in the air. I didn't answer the question. I had heard him, and yet I didn't hear him. I changed the subject almost unconsciously. Every question after that was easy, less revealing and more buoyant, and for the next twenty to thirty minutes, we continued talking about different things: favorite foods, casual interests, things that are just a level above formal greetings and niceties. I don't mind it, and I don't mind it because it is safe and quiet and normal—completely contradictory to how I feel inside of myself. I forget the stifling, closed-in feeling of this room when we talk and it becomes like a sanctuary of serenity, of warm comfort.

C.N. Rowland

At points, the conversation begins to lull into silence. I don't mind that either. I would enjoy his company even without the words, but it is in these quiet moments that I start to recognize the pressure of propriety; when that inner, matronly voice begins to whisper, "You should go now. You have lingered long enough." In these quiet moments I find myself wishing to leave the room, but not because I am done with him. I want to wander outside, find a path beneath a canopy of trees where I can just be, where he can just be. My conscious awareness of the rules, an understanding that was ground into me at an early age, and which society has fostered through adulthood, the need to appear as a proper little lady in the presence of others, in public places, is aggravated by this scholarly setting.

I don't want to be a proper little lady anymore. I want to be an explorer, a mental mechanic, a scientist. I want to ask questions that might seem obscene and unseemly, and I want to ask them because I want to know, society and rules be damned. That hidden liberal never quite bleeds through when I am inside this place, inside this building, contained in these four walls, contained within this body that should be familiar and comfortable, for I have been trapped inside it for thirty years. But I am not comfortable. On the outside, I'm all conservative woman, peering discreetly over my shoulder to see if others are lingering about, if they're wondering why I am here and pressing me into some sort of imagined stereotype: the silly girl fawning over her tutor, an old and well known story. But nothing is ever truly as simple, or as complicated, as it is in stories. This story is not that story, not fully, not really.

My mind has grown enough to know that it is not necessarily him that I am so intensely fascinated with so much as it is the idea that I have of him, the sliver of myself that is reflected in his eyes, unhindered by my own heavy fears and the timidity bought from a tumultuous upbringing; it is the world that he has seen, the things that he has experienced, which I, in my heart, fear I shall never experience, that I crave and desire to know. I want to see behind his eyes. I want to steal into his mind and flip through his memories as though they were photographs pasted into an album. I want to know of the things which I might not ever see, feel, or otherwise taste.

He doesn't seem to register the secret thoughts that I have, but I imagine it is because I keep my air of perfection. My mask is so well made, and I've worn it for so long that people don't even know it is a mask. Maybe he has picked out some of the motivations behind the cool and collected facade and is amused by it, flattered or generally pleased by being a source of interest, but none of that crosses his face in the silence.

I wish he were as easy to read as the books that fill his office; then I could just slide the cover open, devour every word that gave life to detail or action and be done with it, knowing that there was no motivation other than an intense curiosity, and being satisfied, could put down the fixation without regret. But he is not that easy. He is a quietly smiling face with eyes as deep and bright as an ocean, and with the posture of a satiated, old house cat, unconcerned with the curious mouse scampering about him.

The silence has drawn out, making me feel all of the awkwardness that I constantly try to hide, but just before I submit to it, one of us says something else, asks another question and our little containment bubble is instantly re-suspended, but only for a few moments. Someone else approaches the door, sees me sitting in here and passes by, but they don't leave. The invader wanders about in the hall, shuffling papers and while I am slightly distracted by them, I'm still focused enough on his face to see the veil descend; his professor's mask which crashes down immediately and totally obscures the man with whom I was bonding.

I feel that heavy sense of propriety sucking all of the oxygen out of the room and so I push up out of the chair, smiling even while my little, hot air balloon heart begins to deflate in disappointment, begins to settle back upon Earth before I had managed to reach the zenith of some indefinable enjoyment.

I excuse myself with a genuine, "It was really nice talking to you," and manage to duck out without so much as a glance, or glare, at the interloper as I leave, as I wander out of Avalon and trudge out into the parking lot with my mind full of partially satisfied and remarkably unsatisfied curiosities.

Back in the real world, gravity seems heavier and more burdensome. There are a thousand things that I wanted to say but couldn't bring myself to utter, things that will keep me up all night, things that I will say to him at midnight, in a world painted by my imagination.

In the car, driving to work, the broken yellow lines flashing like strobe lights outside of the window, his question comes swimming back to me, the question I had slipped free of with amazing success. I find myself wishing I had answered it. I have this unusual impulse when I'm around him, a keen desire to shake off the shackles of my woman's world and be as a man, speak as a man—all bluntness and force. But how could I tell him about what I write without revealing everything that I am, without exposing all of my flaws, obsessions, passions, secrets, all of things that frighten me, that have me setting myself apart from others, distant and reclusive?

To reveal all of that to someone else, for them to see me like that and turn away from me would be my destruction! But if I could—if I could tell someone everything, and they did not turn away from me—that would be the day I was born, really born into this world.

At work, in-between communicating with vendors and filling out purchase orders, I begin to write in my notebook. I am writing his answer, without any intention of ever showing it to him, but I have to get it out. I have to answer it somehow or it will sit inside of me like a slow poison, gnawing away at me. I pen down the

following:
You asked me what I write about. Here is your answer:

I write of nothing and I write of everything. Every word that I can't bring myself to utter, out of fear, out of misguided notions or beliefs, finds its place on some lonely piece of paper that is doomed to be lost in a shoe box in my closet, or crumpled and thrown away into some random trash bin.

I write of my emotions, which swell like the tides of a great ocean, and can find no escape save through my written words, and even then, only in small degrees. Some of those feelings are so animalistic, so raw and so passionate that I can barely believe they come from me—me who tries so hard to appear proper, to appease and please, to live within the limits that society has forced upon me.

I write because I cannot speak. My voice was lost long ago when I realized that how I see things is not how the majority of others see things. I am a mute, lost in a world of adamant opinions, steel convictions and flawless beliefs. Nothing in my life is so fiercely forged, so black and white.

I write of how I wish I had been born a man, which seems silly in this day and age when women have so many more freedoms than they could have ever imagined in the past, but the ghost of conservatism haunts us still. I am still advised not to go for a walk at night, and to set off on an adventure to some foreign country, unescorted, has been blasted as foolish and ridiculous. I want to be independent of this idea that, because of my sex, I am at the mercy of all. I want to remove the chains of female imprisonment that have conditioned me to bite my tongue, to deny my impulses and my desires.

I want to be a sailor, riding upon the seven seas, dirty and crusted in the salt spray. I want to go to an exotic island and mingle with natives, examine the amazing differences in how

C.N. Rowland

they live, be in peril of being infected with malaria, squat in the woods, dirt under my nails. I want to live life, to take life as a man can take it, but I am not a man. I am a woman, capable only of giving life and living life through whatever means are allowed to me. Allowed, you understand? Even truly independent women have some man in their life telling them what they can and can't, or shouldn't do; they just have more bravery than I possess and only seldom listen.

I write of people that I meet and that inspire me, though most don't even realize that I have contemplated them at all. I have. I think about what makes them fidget with their hands, the way they stand when they are talking to others, shoulders held back or hunched. I watch the way their mouths move, and listen to what they say. I'm interested in most things, and most people, though I might not ever directly plant myself into the sphere of their lives, as I am interested in you. But with you, I have become apparent. I have taken down the veil of shadows in which I hide, at least a little, and I don't normally do that. Something in you inspires me to be more open, more direct. I haven't put my finger on what it is yet, but I am determined to figure it out.

I want to absorb the life you exude, the bluntness and the confidence, the man's world. I want to be a boy in Rome affectionately regarded and doted on with the kind of openness that is allowed only between males. I want to be Charles Darwin, and for you to be my Galapagos Islands. I want to explore you, in every way possible, until I have a full book detailing my discoveries; a book that can be picked up and reread, whenever I please, for the remainder of my days, and then I want to move on, find another adventure, another mystery to explore.

I write to live because it is only through introspection and through retrospection that I can feel as though I am

Darwin's Daughter

connected at all to this world and to this life.

Rereading my letter-long answer to his inquiry, I feel a kind of spiritual transcendence, a kind of freedom that I haven't felt in a long time. Originally, I feared that by writing it all down I would only be giving it more power over me, but the effect was exactly the opposite. I had conquered it through my writing.

Since that meeting, since I spilled my rawness upon a blue lined piece of paper, I have drawn my veil of shadows back down. I have returned to the false world of propriety, but I still watch him from afar with the same fascination burning through my mind and my body. I still linger around corners, alone with my fears, which rival the intensity of my curiosity, and listen as he speaks to the crowd of onlookers, feeling the same, seemingly perpetual pull of his voice.

I am a scientist riding the tides of the ocean, my ship circling the Galapagos, though I know now that my ship will never reach the shore.

Joshua Rigsby *is a Los Angeles-based freelance and fiction writer. Formerly the marketing director for North America's largest organic tea importer, Joshua is a certified tea specialist, and enjoys writing about the history and culture of tea for websites, trade publications, and magazines. Like many of his fellow Angelenos, Joshua is also an avid screenwriter. In recent years he has been fortunate enough to sell scripts to independent producers and film directors, but like many of his fellow screenwriters, he is still waiting for his first film to be produced.*

A Time for Joy

Joshua Rigsby

Fiction

Ford slowly turned his key in the lock of apartment 27, as though he wasn't sure what he'd see when he walked inside. The door creaked in the same way as he walked through and closed it behind him. Everything was the same, as though she had just stepped out for a moment. Clean, well-kept. Couch on one side of the living room. Television set on the other. Dusted. Symmetrical. Primrose. Proper. The rest of the furniture just so. Everything as she had left it except for all the flowers.

It was such an odd feeling.

Ford leaned back against the closed door and sighed. His legs and arms finally relaxed. He loosened the black tie knotted around his neck. He tossed the keys onto the little side table he and Charlotte had bought at that antique store in Montgomery, Alabama. So far away and so long ago.

Joshua Rigsby

Forty years was it? Or thirty-five? He wasn't sure. She was the one who kept the dates and always chastised him for not knowing.

Ford fished the funeral service bulletin out of his suit coat pocket and laid it next to the keys. He would put the little tri-fold paper in a drawer somewhere and forget about it until he accidentally threw it away some day.

He shucked his suit coat and flopped it over a kitchen chair as he made his way to the refrigerator. He would have laid it across the table but for all the flowers. Most were lilies. Resurrection flowers, he was told.

Ford pushed past the covered dishes from friends and relatives, all the tin-foil stuff left over from the wake, and made his way to the very back of the refrigerator to pull out a small white Tupperware capped with a bright red lid. He felt the weight of the dish before opening it and dumping the contents onto a plate.

Fog-gray mashed potatoes covered in oozing brown gravy made way for a hunk of roast beef as it plopped down. Ford turned on the oven and set the plate inside. There would be no more of this, Ford thought to himself, as he listened to the oven tick, hiss, and light with flame. No more meals. This was it. Her last gift to him on her funeral day. How good of her, he thought.

Ford and Charlotte did not have a beautiful relationship. They did not have romantic dinners, or long cruises in the Mediterranean. They didn't walk hand in hand or nuzzle noses as older couples are wont to do. He had tried at first, of course, the way men should, but she met it with a strange sort of resistance. An awkward shrugging off of any outward signs of affection. Eventually he stopped trying all together.

The timer buzzed. Ford pulled out an oven mitt and retrieved his dinner. The roast, the potatoes, the onions, that gravy. The smell. Ah, the smell.

A Time for Joy

Soon he would be able to try those new TV dinners he had seen advertised. Fresh fast food with no cooking necessary. A modern convenience for the modern man. He had been looking forward to the TV dinners for some time, but they would never smell like this. They would never taste like this. Nothing ever did.

Ford pushed the vases aside and ate at the table. When he was done, he pushed his plate away, stuck the tips of his fingers behind his belt, and let in a contented yawn. What to do with all these flowers?

He ran his tongue over his teeth. It would be nice to have a little dessert too.

He rinsed his plate and wandered back into the living room. Still the same. He turned on the television and sat down on the couch as he waited for it to warm up. The station came in clearly. Charlotte's soaps were on. Ford hated soap operas. He always had. He bellyached and groused any time he saw them. Charlotte would turn from the television and raise her eyebrows ever so slightly, and Ford was immediately silenced. Those eyebrows were the masters of the marionette that was his sex life.

Now though, seeing the show felt heavier than it did before. If he changed the channel now it would never change back. There was a finality with anything he did from now on. Every decision he made was one that she would not contribute to. Once he undid something of hers, it would be undone forever. What a strange sensation in his palms as he realized this.

The pang for dessert came to his mouth again. The savory meat and gravy called out for a sweet companion. But what was he supposed to do? He couldn't just up and make himself a pie. That was ridiculous. There was nothing he could do about it then. But... ice cream.

The corner store across the street sold ice cream. He could buy a quart—no—a gallon of ice cream. And not the tri-color

Neapolitan either. Pure, plain vanilla. Ice cream as God meant it to be. Sweet and cold. No surprises.

Ford's face lit with a smile. He would go now.

He put on his slippers, buttoned his pants, and threw himself out the door, his shirttail flapping behind him.

Ford wheeled his legs down the stairs in quick circles, across the width of the Hali Kalani apartment complex and through the side entrance. He trotted across the alleyway, scurried through an abandoned parking lot, and jaywalked across the street to the corner store. His excitement tripled as he flung open the doors and bee-lined to the cold case freezers in the back. He plunged his hands deep into the icy throat of the freezer and came up with a gallon tub of ice cream. Purest white.

The clerk eyed him at the counter.

"Mr. McBride, are you alright?" the clerk asked. "Not to pry, but you look a bit... disheveled."

"I'm doing fine, just fine," Ford said, catching his breath.

"How is your wife doing? I heard that she had taken ill."

"She's splendid. That's $1.25 I believe?"

"Yessir."

"Well, there you are. Keep the change. Tell Bernard I said hello."

"Thank you sir. I will," the clerk said, but Ford was already gone.

Inside apartment 27, Ford scooped two generous helpings into a bowl, and found, much to his delight, that the gallon tub fit precisely into his icebox. He had to take all the other frozen food out of the icebox first, of course, but he hadn't the slightest intention of eating any of those things to begin with.

He set the bowl on his coffee table, and advanced toward the television cautiously. He turned it on, and waited for the picture

A Time for Joy

to show again. The soap opera was nearly over now. He placed a trembling hand on the dial. He paused for a moment, took a breath, and turned.

The channel clicked and changed. That was it. He had done it. It was done.

He sat on the couch and picked up his ice cream, his eyes far away, thinking about the origins of things, and where she was, and if she was happy there.

He was relieved when she had finally died, for her sake and for himself. No more pain for either of them. He had wept in the intervening days, and at the funeral. He would miss her. Now, though, it was time to laugh like he hadn't wanted to laugh since he was a child. Doubled over, wheezing, breathless laughter. That was what he wanted. Pent up for decades, he would let them all free at once.

Tomorrow it would be time to pull down those oppressively dark curtains. He always loved the light, pure and unadorned. Today, though, they could stay. It was how she had left them for him.

Terry Cobb *resides with her husband on a farm in north central Missouri, where she gardens, writes, and photographs whatever catches her eye. Her short stories have appeared in* Well Versed 2014 Anthology, The Binnacle Ultra-Short 2013 Edition, *and* Downstate Story E-zine 2012, *and her flash fiction has won awards from The Pike's Peak Women Writers, Green River Writers, Saturday Writers, and the Springfield Missouri Writers Guild. Her devotionals have been published in* The Upper Room *and* The Secret Place. *She has also written blog articles for* Women on Writing Speak Out Friday *and* Capper's Heart of the Home *websites. Terry's gardening blog is at <u>www.whatsinyourgarden.wordpress.com.</u>*

Break a Leg

Terry Cobb

Fiction

Lana bit her lip and held her breath as she listened to Ray's introduction. She wished the stage manager would look up from his damn clipboard and call out, "break a leg." But since she'd turned seventy, no one has dared to say such a thing. Fighting these butterflies was silly. It's not like the Dubuque Music Hall, or whatever-the-hell they called the building, was Caesars Palace. Yet, it had been ten years since her last performance in front of a half-filled theater in Las Vegas—ten years since promoters had pronounced her too old to be sexy.

"Please give a warm hometown welcome to the Hollywood legend who never forgot her Midwestern roots. A siren of film and stage who has so graciously come out of retirement to help us raise funds to keep the arts alive in Dubuque. Here's the lady who needs no last name: Lana!"

The crowd burst into applause as trumpets blared a fanfare. Lana stepped onto the stage and into the hot, bright lights trained on her surgically-stretched face. She opened her arms to embrace the crowd and blew them kisses. The spotlight, the applause, the love. God, how she had missed this. Butterflies be damned. She was feisty and sexy and twenty years younger. "Lana, Star of Stage and Screen" was back!

Although she hadn't rehearsed any steps, Lana danced across the stage toward a bemused Ray to tease and toy with him. In a playful move, she tried to swipe Ray's microphone when he wasn't looking but overreached and her right knee buckled. She stumbled and reeled on the platform heels the stage director had begged her not to wear. Ray's left arm swooped around her waist, and he strode, half-carrying her, to the front of the stage as if it had all been choreographed.

Still hugging her, he whispered through his tight smile, "Do you want me to stay with you?"

The question incensed her more than the pain in her knee. This yokel imported from Des Moines obviously didn't appreciate the skills of a veteran performer such as herself. She planted a big kiss on his cheek and pushed him toward the wings as she laughed and waved him good-bye.

She turned to the audience and flipped a strand of Lady Clairol blonde hair, her signature gesture, as she twisted and pivoted so they could admire her slim figure, accentuated by her flowing white gown that dipped drastically in the front. She bowed again and kept her right leg bared in the precariously high slit of her skirt. After all, this is what the audience had come to see, the '70s sex symbol who had made millions for the tabloids with her sultry looks and affairs. She'd give them a night to remember.

The band quieted, her cue to address the audience. "It's great to be back in Dubuque! Oh, how I've missed the wonderful people of Iowa!"

Break a Leg

She nodded her thanks for the additional ripple of applause. "Let's have some fun with a little song that I used to sing in my Vegas shows." She turned to the band and flipped her hair. "Hit it, boys!"

The band broke into "Delta Dawn," a real crowd-pleaser in Lana's heyday. Fighting the pain in her knee, she wobbled on her heels as she tried to prance along the edge of the stage and engage the audience. The stage lights kept her from seeing much beyond the first two rows, but what she did see troubled her: crossed arms, frowns, shaking heads and whispers. Midwesterners had always been more uptight than her Vegas crowds, but these people were rude.

Lana clapped her hands when she got to the chorus and shouted to the audience to join in. Although none did, she pretended they were into it and emoted the words. The crowd's continued lack of interest rattled her. She thought the band must be doing something distracting until she noticed a lady in the front row nudge her seat mate, point at Lana's legs, and giggle.

Unable to resist looking, Lana glanced down at a run in her stocking. It broke her concentration and she garbled a few words. She got half-a-beat off from the band and jumped in late when she missed her cue to sing the chorus which then hurried the line and ruined the tempo. The music, so loud and fast, made the room sway as sweat ran down Lana's neck and into her cleavage. Breathless and fighting to keep from fainting, she bowed her head and dropped the microphone to her side while the band continued to play. The people on the front row murmured and exchanged worried looks.

Ray rushed onstage laughing and clapping. He hugged her and exclaimed to the crowd, "Isn't she wonderful? C'mon let's have a big round of applause for Lana!"

Tears filled her eyes as Lana leaned into Ray and whispered, "I can't finish like this."

"One more time! Let's everybody do the chorus!" Ray shouted. Keeping his arm around her waist, he turned to the bandleader behind him, mouthed instructions and held up one finger. Lana and the audience followed his lead, and the band ended the song with a flourish.

"There you are my friends, the lovely Lana!"

The applause was muted but polite. Lana bowed her head to the crowd like a vanquished warrior. Determined to hide her tears, she closed her eyes and bit her lip. As she turned to leave, a tall, thin man from the second row stood and shouted, "Bravo Lana!"

She blew him a kiss and limped off the stage leaning on Ray but holding her head high.

Ramona Scarborough *is the author of* Stranger Friends, *a collection of short stories, two historical fiction novels,* The Autograph Book *and its sequel,* Anna's Diary, *two romance novellas,* Rivals *and* A Moment in Time, *and a suspense novella,* Soft Kill. *For two years in a row, her stories have placed in the top 50 out of thousands of entries in the Writer's Digest Writing competition. Last year, she won the 2nd place Gracie Award for* Unsweetened Revenge, *won two contests for Oregon Women's Report and placed stories in three anthologies.*

Coast to Coast

Ramona Scarborough

Fiction

Albert covered ten miles today, five this morning and five this afternoon. He whistled under his breath and ignored his burning feet. The toothpick he'd stuck in his mouth when starting out was chewed to shreds, and he spit the wood fragments into the gutter. He'd tried gum, but it didn't absorb the pain as well.

He'd mark his progress on the large print map of the United States as soon as he removed his tennis shoes, mopped the perspiration off his bald head and sopped up the sweat streaming down the wrinkled gullies on his face.

His trembling fingers traced Highway 30 between Kearney and Grand Island, Nebraska, only about fifteen more miles to Grand Island. He looked back across the page to where he had started approximately 1,673 miles away—Lincoln City, Oregon. He'd been walking seven days a week for six and a half months.

He sat down on the bed and opened his cell phone.

"Bert here."

"Yah, how many today?" John said.

"Ten, another day and a half and I'll be in Grand Island."

John leaned over in his recliner and rubbed his bum knee as if he had walked the ten miles.

"That's good, Bert, I'll be trackin' it on my map after supper."

"I've gotta rest now, but I'll call you in the morning with all the details."

Was it eight years ago, this harebrained idea had first formed in his mind? Yep, he'd been walking his mail route and stuffing Mrs. March's myriad travel brochures into her mailbox. Mrs. March had told him her next trip included a ride up the Yang see River in China.

Albert had lived in Salem, Oregon all his life and only been in three states, Washington, Oregon and California.

All these miles I've walked going nowhere. Why, I probably have walked across the U.S. and back. I could! When I retire, I could!

Albert lay down on top of the bedspread and opened his book, *A Roadside History of Nebraska*. He thumbed through to the section on Grand Island. "Once the homeland of the Pawnee, Omaha and Otoe Indians."

He'd never heard of the Otoe's. *Great, another subject to look up on the Internet tonight.*

The other book on Nebraska was a federal writer's project and gave information about points of interest in the area. He'd tell John about the surrounding country, fields of corn, sugar beets and alfalfa. In Grand Island, John might be interested in the auctions held at the Livestock Commission Company Market, or the original Station for the Union Pacific Railroad, whose tracks still bisected the city at an angle contrary to most Nebraska cities.

Oh, yes, he'd find plenty of material to divert John from his present condition; a man bound to his Lazy Boy by surgeries and overweight.

Albert remembered the first time he'd mentioned to John that he wanted to walk across the United States. They'd been sorting mail for their respective routes and stashing it into their heavy mailbags.

"When you planning on doing this?" was all he said.

Bess, Albert's wife, had been matter of fact too. She wiped her hands on her apron and smiled at him.

"Knowing you, you got it all planned out already."

Bess was right. After being married for thirty-two years there wasn't much she didn't know about him. But Bess turned out to be the reason he had started late and in a much different way than his plans called for. Still, this venture was one of the most exciting happenings in his whole life. He couldn't have done it any other way, remembering all the years that Bessie had looked at him as if he had a superman costume hidden under his postman's uniform. She had made stroganoff that made your mouth water. Just thinking about the tender beef and mushrooms swimming in sour cream sauce made his mouth water. Oh, and her yeast biscuits, browned on top with soft middles smeared with real butter and raspberry jam. When no children appeared as they hoped, Bess said, "We have each other."

The year he'd signed up for Social Security was when he'd first noticed a change in Bess. He'd bought her a dress that she had seen in the catalog and a new-fangled set of pots and pans for their anniversary. She set the double boiler on the stove to steam broccoli and forgot to put water in the lower pan. The bottom melted into silver tears on the burner. He was far more concerned about her tears. That was just the beginning. She began wandering away from him in her mind and then literally, causing them to be housebound for fear she might get lost.

For seven years, he'd called his friend, John every day. After retirement, John's health had prevented him from fishing and camping, his favorite activities. He knew all the scores for TV sports, and he and Albert liked to grouse over White House blunders on the news.

The nurse from Health Services told Albert he should move Bess to a nursing home. He didn't listen until he slipped in the bathtub and broke his arm. Fairwood Village, an assisted living community, was in the same neighborhood as their house. The expense would drain Albert's income, his Social Security and pension, but he realized he wasn't able to properly care for Bess anymore.

Albert roamed aimlessly from one room to another when he returned home from moving Bess to a small room on the first floor. He'd been cooking all the meals for years, but he didn't feel hungry. He reached for his phone.

"Bert here, I've got her settled."

"You know, Bert, I've been thinking." There was a long pause on John's end. "Maybe now that you don't have Bess at home, you could do that walk across the country." Albert spread the map across the kitchen table. He pulled out a tablet and began writing hastily, Highway 101 for three miles, Highway 18 toward Salem.

That evening, he mapped the whole trip, from coast to coast, from Lincoln City to Norfolk, Virginia, when his stomach growled. He opened the refrigerator and pulled out roast beef from the deli and slathered some mayonnaise on wheat bread. He flipped open a can of beer and moved the map over and wolfed down his sandwich.

As soon as his stomach stopped yelling, his conscience began.

How could you abandon Bessie? OK, sometimes she's not sure who you are, but how could you not be there when she does? Would those overworked nurses take good care of her? Not likely.

Albert slumped in his chair. *How could he have been so selfish? His dream would have to die like the wilting houseplants he kept forgetting to water.*

The idea, however, kept cropping up like the new sprouts in his garden. One day, when pulling his old Buick into a parking spot at Fairwood Village, he absently looked at the odometer. It was about

Coast to Coast

two and a half miles from home to where Bess waited for him in her room she shared with Mrs. Ashford.

"That's it!" He shouted aloud, striking his palm on the steering wheel. He told Bess all about it, holding her hands, while she smiled without understanding. Somewhere inside though, she must have sensed his excitement.

"It's my Albert," she said, turning to Mrs. Ashford.

And so it began, coast to coast, Albert walking five miles in the morning and five in the afternoon, back and forth, two and half miles there and back. The next day he fed Bess breakfast in the Deschutes National Forest, and dinner another day in Bend, Oregon. He combed her unruly curls down in Nampa, Idaho and lugged a bag of her laundry home on his shoulder as he trudged toward Rock Springs, Wyoming. He drove to the library every week extracting his journey from the photographs and pages of books.

"John, Bert here, I'm calling from Saint Louis, Missouri."

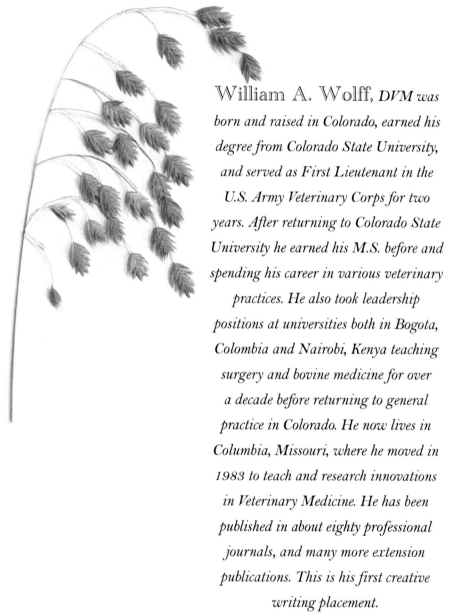

William A. Wolff, *DVM was born and raised in Colorado, earned his degree from Colorado State University, and served as First Lieutenant in the U.S. Army Veterinary Corps for two years. After returning to Colorado State University he earned his M.S. before and spending his career in various veterinary practices. He also took leadership positions at universities both in Bogota, Colombia and Nairobi, Kenya teaching surgery and bovine medicine for over a decade before returning to general practice in Colorado. He now lives in Columbia, Missouri, where he moved in 1983 to teach and research innovations in Veterinary Medicine. He has been published in about eighty professional journals, and many more extension publications. This is his first creative writing placement.*

Divergent Directions

William A. Wolff

Creative Nonfiction

By the summer of 1947, the war had been over for two years and the economy was booming. Veterans were getting good jobs, many in home and small business construction. Everything was looking up.

My dad was a successful land developer, home building contractor, and real estate broker in Denver and the surrounding area. His dad, my grandfather, H. G. Wolff, a pioneer developer in the Denver area for many years, had left him a seemingly endless supply of mostly empty land ripe for development. Thanks to low-cost financing made possible by the G.I. Bill, veterans and their families were buying reasonably priced homes in record numbers. Schools and shopping centers sprang up to serve the new neighborhoods in record time, which only added to the construction boom.

Sometimes the materials used and quality of construction

were substandard, and demand was so great that faulty houses were fairly common. My father, however, was determined to treat veterans well and provided quality at every step of procurement and construction, plus warranty on construction and appliances.

When my brother Brad returned from the South Pacific, he joined Dad and added great ideas, an outgoing personality, and some much-needed humor to the company. He was a natural businessman. He and Dad were a compatible team.

In the spring of 1947, I was a junior in high school, already looking forward to graduation next year. I worked for Brad hauling bricks, shoveling dirt, mixing cement, and generally cleaning up. Colorado seasons are summer, autumn, winter and Mud—and May of 1947 was the height of the Mud season. Despite the "mud-outs," I enjoyed being outside, enjoyed the physical work. My five dollars an hour was good money! College money. And as things would work out, or rather, wouldn't work out between Dad and me, I would need college money.

By the time I entered my teens, Dad and I had a long "history." We just didn't get along. As a kid I obeyed him, but sullenly and often only after being severely disciplined. I was a sickly kid as a result of contracting scarlet fever in 1938 when I was eight. In those long ago days—no penicillin or sulfa drugs—children died from scarlet fever. Mom told me years later that Dad resented me, was scornful about my being a "sickly kid." I became a rotten, spoiled nuisance, nasty to both parents, but I took most of my resentment out on Mom because I was frightened of Dad.

When I turned thirteen, my parents had had enough. Our neighbors, the Whatleys, owned a ranch in Western Colorado and my parents cut a deal with them. I would work on their ranch the coming summer as a chore boy. That summer I discovered who I was, or, rather, who I wanted to become. I grew up, very painfully at first. The Whatleys were stern taskmasters, brooked

Divergent Directions

no back talk or swearing, demanded performance and respect for others. For the first time I learned the soul-cleansing value of hard physical labor. And, the greatest bonus of all, I fell in love with ranch life. I milked cows, harnessed and drove mules, slopped hogs, dressed chickens for Sunday dinner, and joyfully rode old Buck in the long evenings after milking. I also learned humility. When I returned home at the end of the summer, I had changed. My newly discovered knowledge of and respect for animals had sent me in a direction my father had never imagined possible.

After that junior high summer at the Whatley Ranch, I worked summers until my third year of high school at the Painter Hereford Company, a large ranching operation about sixty-five miles east of Denver at Roggen, Colorado. There I met and worked with Dr. Cooper, a veterinarian who visited the ranch frequently. His professionalism and his dedication to the animals placed in his care convinced me that I wanted to be a veterinarian.

Other events conspired to push me along. Mom and Dad divorced soon after the summer I spent at the Whatley Ranch. Mom bought a small farm near Arvada, a farming community northwest of Denver. I moved with her, spent most of my free time there, but saw Dad at least once a week. Luckily, the Arvada Veterinary Clinic provided me another opportunity to work with veterinarians, Drs. Vyrle Stauffer and Gail Gilbert. They were wonderful men, dedicated to their profession, unselfish with their long hours spent helping animals and their owners. The more time I spent around veterinarians, the more I observed their excellence of character and the abilities they displayed, the more I wanted to be like them, to be one of them.

But my father had other plans. As the summer of 1947 approached and I was making plans to return to the Painter Ranch, Dad appeared one day at the construction site where I was working. "Bill," he said, "I have a friend in Boulder who is a professor at Colorado University and I would like for us to meet with him and discuss enrolling you there next year."

Our moment of open conflict had arrived. We had discussed college once before in general terms, and the idea seemed okay. But I knew what I wanted to do. Hoping to temper the situation, I replied. "Sure, I'll go with you to get some ideas, Dad, but I'm going to enroll at Colorado A & M. After two years of pre-vet I hope to get into vet school." My father's face froze. I ignored the warning signal and continued. "We've talked about this before and this is my goal."

He turned as if to walk away, then turned back. "You haven't learned much about loyalty and obedience. You have really changed since you worked for Barney Whatley. I'm sorry we ever sent you there!" Knowing I had said more than enough, I remained quiet. Dad rolled on. "Okay, if you go to "cow college" I won't pay a dime for your college education. And, understand this, I will never permit you to enter vet school!"

That, I couldn't let pass. "How the hell can you prevent me from going to vet school?" I spat it out.

He spat back, "You'll find out if you follow that path!!"

I couldn't quit on that note. "What's this about loyalty and obedience? I'm not disloyal to you by not being interested in a career in business. I don't like golf and I'm not going to suffer through any more dinners at the Cherry Hills Country Club. Why am I being disobedient by wanting to be a veterinarian? This is my life!"

He looked very sad, and asked, quietly, "Bill, with all the great opportunities out there these days, why do you choose veterinary medicine?"

I had cooled down as well. I couldn't leave things on a sour note. "Dad, look at my history, please. My path has been in this direction since my first contact with Dr. Cooper. I really admire your hard work and honesty as a businessman, and I know that you are well respected in Denver. But I have chosen another course."

Divergent Directions

In the spring of 1948 with graduation approaching, I applied for admission to Colorado A & M in Pre-Veterinary Medicine. I was accepted. A letter from the registrar with registration details made it all very real, very close. Mom was pleased. For several years I had talked at length with her about my experience with Dr. Cooper and my intention of going to veterinary school. She had come by the ranch to see the place and visit the Painter family. Dad had never shown any interest. Coward that I was, I told Dad about the letter of acceptance over the phone. He repeated his threat that he would never permit me to attend "cow college." And that, as far as he was concerned, was the end of the discussion.

Brimming with defiance, I set off in the fall to begin my new life. As expected, Dad didn't offer any help, but Mom and I scraped together enough money for first quarter registration and books (about a hundred and fifty dollars—a paltry sum by today's standards). My first two years were difficult. I struggled through algebra—who doesn't?—and trigonometry. I flunked Sociology and managed only a shaky B average. To stay in school I did what most of my friends were doing; I worked at any job I could get. Anything to make a buck or two at the princely rate of seventy-five cents an hour. I sold books at the Campus Shop, cleaned kennels at the vet school, cleaned stalls at the horse barns on the Ag campus, picked cherries at the orchards north of Fort Collins and worked as a steward at a sorority house. Side benefits as a steward at the Tri Delt house included food and dating sorority girls. The girls had more money than we did, so we let them pay for a burger if they insisted. And, a pitcher of beer at Smitty's was twenty-five cents. Life was good.

But always, deep inside, I felt a gnawing uncertainty. From the start I had known that admission to pre-veterinary medicine was but the first step on a long road. Two years after enrolling, I learned I was one of three hundred applicants determined to enroll in the School of Veterinary Medicine in the fall of 1950. Only sixty would be admitted. My mother continued to be supportive. I had tried to keep in touch with Dad during that first year of college, but he was distant whenever I called. I sent him a birthday card but got no response. Phone calls became fewer; finally, they stopped altogether.

Interviews to select the veterinary medicine class for the fall of 1950 began in April. The panel before which I sat was composed of five of the most prominent—and most daunting—men in veterinary medicine: Dean Floyd Cross, medicine; Dr. James Farquharson, surgery; Dr. Rue Jensen, pathology; Dr. Lloyd Moss, small animal medicine; and Dr. Robert Davis, anatomy.

They were courteous, but they asked pointed questions and expected answers. It was a hot day, no air conditioning, no fan, just an open window. Before long, I was sitting in a pool of my own sweat and my deodorant ran out. They knew everything about me. That at thirteen I had worked as a chore boy on the Whatley Ranch and later worked with Dr. Cooper at the Painter Ranch worked in my favor. But I had flunked Sociology with prejudice, and my grade point average was hardly stellar. When they noted that I had been cited by the Fort Collins police for "pissing" a stop sign, I tried to explain that I had been cited for passing a stop sign, but my explanation was drowned out by laughter. The atmosphere lightened and I became a bit hopeful when they saw the humor in the situation.

Then the interview took an unexpected turn. I mentioned that a muleskinner on the Whatley Ranch had taken me in tow and taught me a few things about mules. On and on I went, talking with more and more animation about mules: how they were smarter than horses, how they wouldn't hurt themselves if they were caught in barbed wire, how they wouldn't overeat and founder, and were stronger than horses. Dr. Moss countered. He hated mules, had grown up with them in Missouri and had the scars to show for it. But I was on a roll. "Maybe the mules," I suggested, "had been

Divergent Directions

mistreated." Oops! I thought I was dead, but Dr. Moss agreed. He admitted that the mules he knew had at times been mistreated. In turn, I admitted that mules could be mean. The big jack at the Whatley Ranch had caused me to have to shoot my favorite horse at the ranch. Black Jack kicked old Buck and broke his leg. Dr. Moss and I chatted a while longer about favorite animals. He started on Blue Tick Hounds until another panelist wanted to get a word in edgewise.

"I sweated bullets for a couple of weeks before I received a brief note that I was accepted for the first year of the "Professional Course of Veterinary Medicine."

I called Mom and she was thrilled. Calling my distant father was more difficult. When I finally summoned up my courage, Bylle, my new stepmom, answered the phone. Dad was out; could she take a message? Days later, I talked at last with my father, told him the news, and asked if I could stop by to visit. That evening, he was cordial, but distant. He offered me a drink, which I accepted with considerable relief. Bylle wasn't there. I wished she had been. I wanted to meet her and thought her presence would soften the inevitable explosion. I told him of my hopes for veterinary school, my search for a summer job. Small talk. Minutes later the floodgates opened and familiar waters rushed over me. I had made a bad decision, he claimed, but he wasn't surprised I had been admitted. "Any loser can get into vet school," he proclaimed. And then, one more time, he issued his familiar ultimatum: "You will not go to veterinary school."

Toward the middle of the summer Dad called and told me that we were going to Fort Collins to meet with the veterinary school admissions panel. "What's this all about?" I asked.

"You'll find out," was all he offered by way of reply. He gave me the date and time; I gave him directions to the Dean's office.

Hoping to prepare myself, I arranged for an earlier meeting with Dean Cross. "We received a letter from your father," he told me, "and he is determined that you are not going to veterinary school. So far as we are concerned, our decision is final, and I believe yours is also. We will meet with him only if you agree."

I agreed, but I was apprehensive. Dad was—to say the least—unpredictable.

Half sick with nerves, I was already at the Dean's office when my father arrived. I asked him why he wanted to meet. "You have made a terrible decision about your future," he told me one more time, "and I'm going to correct it."

What seemed an eternity later, Dr. Cross and Dr. Davis emerged from the dean's office. After handshakes all around, we went in and sat down. Someone served coffee. Another hot day, still no air conditioning. The Dean started by reading my father's letter aloud. "Mr. Wolff," he began, "you say in your letter that Bill really doesn't know what he wants and that he has been unduly influenced by a few veterinarians with whom he has been associated. You say that you have never heard of anything veterinarians accomplished in the medical or scientific fields." For a moment, Dr. Cross fell silent. "Mr. Wolff, have you heard of Tuberculosis or Brucellosis, Rabies, or Rocky Mountain Spotted Fever? Veterinarians are responsible for control of these communicable diseases and many more. Did you know that all meat and dairy products are inspected by veterinarians for disease and chemical contamination?" For several minutes Dean Cross continued talking about the accomplishments of the veterinary profession since the mid-1800s, the rapid expansion of vaccine technology mostly due to veterinary scientists, the role of veterinarians in developing pharmaceuticals and vaccines for human beings.

My father was not impressed. "Billy is just a kid. He doesn't really know what he wants."

Calling me Billy got my adrenalin up. "Its my life, not yours!" I think I shouted. Dean Cross brought us back to civility. The admissions board, he reminded my father, was proud of the fact that the school had a reputation for accepting and graduating the very best. And I had been accepted.

Obviously uncomfortable and frustrated, Dad blurted out the sort of thing I most feared: "Well, I don't know a single veterinarian who belongs to a country club!" Humiliated, I sank into my chair, would have disappeared through the floor had it been possible. The men at the table stared. A long silence settled over the room.

Then Dean Cross turned to me. "Bill, will you be in our next freshman class?" I couldn't speak, but nodded my head yes.

Exactly how that meeting ended, I don't remember. Ashamed for my father and for me, I had retreated deep into myself. But that fall I did enter the freshman class. No one but myself, Dr. Cross and Dr. Davis knew of my problem with Dad—not my classmates, not the other professors. No one, except Mom. I had sent her a letter describing Dad's behavior. Her response was simple; "You must make amends with your father. You will have to lead because he won't. You must prove to him, to me, and to yourself that you are above the petty disagreements and stubbornness that have separated you two for years. It's up to you."

The letter I eventually sent to my father was brief: apologies for disrespect, for stubbornness, for all the things I thought I should confess to, but didn't really believe I was guilty of. Though I found it patently insincere, I sent it anyway. For a long time, nothing came back. And then, one night halfway into the first quarter, Dad called. He wanted to come to Fort Collins and take me to dinner. Knowing Dad's tastes, I asked my employer, Harry Dimmit at the Campus Shop, about the best restaurant in town. "The Northern Hotel," he told me with a wink; "it's the only restaurant in town with white tablecloths."

He picked me up, and to my surprise and relief, Bylle was with him. All around were smiles and 'glad-to-see-you's. Bylle was very gracious, Dad was—cordial. Dinner was uneventful, lots of small talk. Dad and I talked about a new home development in Fort

William A. Wolff

Collins in which he had an interest; Bylle asked questions about school. She seemed genuinely interested. We shared a pleasant evening and parted for once on an agreeable note.

After dinner, they dropped me off at the converted garage in which I lived. To my surprise, as I was getting out of the car, Dad handed me an envelope. Looking inside, I found a check for $350 and a note: "Make this last." I sent a note of thanks the next day. I was thankful, of course, for the money that would make my life so much easier. I did make it last. My mother's advice helped break the barrier between two stubborn people. Dad's gift was also an open door for reconciliation, which we both moved cautiously through later in the year. And it was good. And, I never joined a country club.

Lili Flanders *is a graduate of the Juilliard School of Drama and the MFA Program for Writers at Warren Wilson College. She lives in Los Angeles and Truro, Cape Cod. She and her husband, actor Peter Mackenzie, have three children. Her fiction and creative nonfiction have appeared or are upcoming in* Pearl, New Plains Review *and* The Healing Muse. *Her flash fiction has appeared in* Vestal Review, Foundling Review, Writer Advice *and* New Millennium Writings. *Her flash story, "Intersection, Late Afternoon" won* Vestal Review's *Ten Years in Flash Fiction contest. Her flash story, "Ebb Tide" won third place in this year's* Writer Advice *Flash Prose Contest, and received an honorable mention in* New Millennium Writings' *Short-Short Fiction Contest.*

Flight

Lili Flanders

Creative Nonfiction

I get regular massages. No one begrudges me this; in fact, I'm applauded. It's part of the "taking care of me so I can take care of Niles" program. I indulge in naps, too.

When I visit school, colleagues tell me how good I look. I don't know if they're comparing the way I look now to the way I looked when I was teaching, or if they mean I look better than they would expect me to…considering. It's the naps, I say. With a couple of trusted coworkers I elaborate: it's the naps, and no longer having to attend faculty meetings.

I believe in the caregiver's self-care program, but I'm also self-conscious about it. Maybe a mother whose son is undergoing cancer treatment shouldn't look rested. I feel uneasy about any benefits I enjoy because of Niles's illness—not just the naps and massages, but a heightened sense of purpose, too, a strange exhilaration that might actually be panic but feels more like vigor. There's a new and essential energy to our days that is as vivid as the ache I feel for what Niles has to go through, and as potent as the constant fear of what lies ahead.

It's possible, however, that I'm not as rested as I look. I've become convinced—on a level that is not exactly on par with reality, but exists on a congruent plane—that I'm becoming an angel. The first sense I had of this transformation was in the Outpatient Cancer Center's main waiting area. Niles and I were sitting in chairs facing the big fish tank. I was holding the thick plastic coaster that would vibrate when it was Niles's turn to check in. A child with the sad, patient eyes of an old dog sat in a stroller opposite us. She might have been three years old, no more than five. A pink beanie covered her hairless head. She was eating raisins, probing into the little red box with her index finger and carefully bringing each wrinkled fruit to her mouth. When she noticed that I was watching her, she returned my look with a disinterested gaze. I opted not to turn away or smile, but simply to meet her eyes, to match her neutrality and openness with my own. That's when I felt it: a warmth filling my body, as though I were a conduit, as though energy were passing through me to her. The warmth was concentrated in my shoulder blades.

I tell my masseuse about this at my next appointment. "Masseuse" is a limiting title for Rochelle; she's a gifted healer. Because she regularly converses with spirits and can see energy-sucking lizards attached to people's heads, I figure she won't be freaked out by the news that I'm becoming an angel. I mention the sensitivity in my shoulder blades and try to explain the sensation I had while looking at the little girl in the stroller.

"This is weird," I say, "but I know what color my wings are— gray, like a young seagull's."

Rochelle massages my shoulder blades, loosens up the muscles in my back so that my wings can grow. At the end of our session, she suggests that I see an energy specialist. She gives me the phone number of a woman who was an important guide in her own journey as a healer. I take the number gratefully. There's a freedom to being an extremist; you're no longer bound by the usual conventions and considerations. You're open to possibilities that previously might have seemed frightening or absurd.

The energy specialist lives in a cottage behind a stucco bungalow in Hollywood. I park my car and pass through a wooden gate, following a driveway with a strip of dried grass down the middle of it, to a miniature white clapboard home with bright blue trim. I knock on the door and a middle-aged woman answers. She's round, with frizzy blond hair, and stands about four feet six. A munchkin healer in a fairy-tale cottage. This, for reasons that will soon become unclear to me, I find reassuring.

She invites me inside. There is a lot of lace. Angel effigies hang in doorways, in windows and from lampshades. Clearly, I've come to the right place. The specialist asks me to sit on the sofa and I sink into chintz. She climbs onto a chenille-covered armchair opposite me. I tell her about Niles and the little girl in the stroller and my wing sprouts. She doesn't smile or nod as I expect; she doesn't welcome me into the tribe of messengers. Instead, she looks wary, slightly dissatisfied.

"Your aura is flat," she says. Then she wiggles to the edge of her armchair, hops to the floor, and leads me into an alcove between the tiny living room and yellow-tiled kitchen. She tells me to remove my shoes, but to leave the rest of my clothes on, and to lie face-up on the massage table that takes up almost every inch of the space. While I get settled, she lights gardenia-scented candles. Before she turns on the atmospheric soundtrack, she warns me that she might make strange noises as she extracts negative energy from my body. I close my eyes. Music that sounds as though it's created from found objects fills the room.

The energy specialist begins at my head, gently placing her hands on either side of my skull. After a few moments, her fingers begin to tremble and twitch, as though they've connected to a faint electrical current. She clears her throat. Then she moves her hands down to my shoulders and slides a palm between my shoulder blades. Soon, she begins to cough in a ragged, back-of-the-throat way, like someone trying to bring up mucus. I thought I was growing wings, but maybe it's just bad energy sticking to my bones like phlegm.

Floating in a half-sleep, aware still of the music that now sounds like tinkling glass, I find myself entering a scene from *The English Patient*, a novel I read a decade ago. I was nine months pregnant then, waiting day to day for our daughter to be born. The novel seemed to me less written than dreamed onto the page, and I read it in my own dream-state of fatigue and anticipation. I've seen the film version since then, but the images and sensations that come to me now are not from the screen but my own experience of reading the book. I recognize the dark desert, the dance of flame, the tinkling of glass bottles from my own imagination. Sense memories surface from deep storage. I am the English patient, being tended to by gentle strangers. I hear roughhewn words murmured in an unknown language. I smell musky cloth, herbs, wood smoke. I feel myself being lifted. I'm interested and calm. The energy specialist coughs again, sniffs, coughs.

An hour later, we are once again sitting opposite each other in the living room. The specialist asks me how I feel. I smile and bob my head.

"Your aura is bright now. It's radiating energy out the top of your head. Do you feel it?"

I tell her about Ondaatje's scene in the desert, how images and sensations came back to me while I was on the table, as though they were my own memories.

"I felt a lot of fear in you," she says.

I write her a check and she walks me to the door. We're both smiling now; we've come to an understanding.

"Thanks," I say, "I'll be back."

But I won't, and I'm convinced she knows this as well as I do. She will not indulge me my wings and I cannot pretend to feel energy radiating out of the top of my head. I would like to; I'm hungry for transformation, but the afternoon has suddenly become banal. I'm aware of an odor of cooked broccoli beneath the smoky bouquet of candles.

I leave feeling not so much disappointed as sober. I know that wherever Niles's illness takes us, or whatever transformation I undergo will not be fast, or easy, or magical.

Jan Bowman, *Winner of the 2011 Roanoke Review Fiction Award, Jan's stories have been nominated for Pushcart Prizes, Best American Short Stories, and a Pen/O'Henry award. Glimmer Train named a story as Honorable Mention in the November 2012 Short Story Awards for New Writers. Her stories have been finalists for the 2013 Broad River Review RASH Award for Fiction, 2013 finalists in the Phoebe Fiction Contest and 2012 "So To Speak" Fiction Contest.*

Jan's fiction has appeared in numerous publications including Big Muddy, The Broadkill Review, Third Wednesday, Minimus, Buffalo Spree (97), Folio, The Potomac Review, Musings, Potato Eyes and others. She is working on two collections of short stories while shopping for a publisher for a completed story collection, Mermaids & Other Stories. She has nonfiction publications in Atticus Review, Trajectory and Pen-in-Hand. She writes a weekly blog of "Reflections" on the writing life and posts regular interviews with writers and publishers. Learn more at: www.janbowmanwriter.com.

Rabbits

Jan Bowman

Fiction

Early in the eighties when we had the chance to buy land and build a house in upper state South Carolina, we grabbed it, although my wife, Alice, who was particularly close to her family, dreaded the thought of leaving Charleston. "It's only four hours away," I reminded her, "not too far to drive down for a weekend." This was after the incident happened to our daughter, Mary Ann. A crazy boy in her eighth-grade art class went on a rampage. He slashed out with sharp pointed scissors—a random act, they said—and cut a gash across the side of her cheek while she sat drawing a charcoal sketch of a pony. The wound healed leaving only a faint scar, but that was the moment when I realized the world was going mad and I needed to get my five kids to some quiet safe place, away from violence.

Perhaps it was the missing connections to nature that caused people, crazed by noise and traffic, to be unpredictably violent, even in a sleepy southern city like Charleston.

After the builder finished the house and barn in January, I went with the movers a week ahead to get the house organized while Alice and the kids stayed with her mother. The builder had gone bankrupt before he'd finished the landscaping around the porch and deck; the meadow behind the house was rough and muddy in the gray light of a winter afternoon. I made plans to plant trees and shrubs by spring. But finally we had a house large enough for our family, built the way we wanted it, just as I had promised Alice when we first married.

My four daughters had mixed reactions to the move. Cindy and Mary Ann, our oldest daughters were angry about leaving their friends. And our two younger daughters, Joan and Lisa didn't want to leave their grandmother. But they all calmed down when I agreed to buy a pony.

I located a farmer who sold us a young gelding pony and a calf; he even sent over a flock of chickens in a crate. Our boy, Clint, barely three years old, was intrigued and terrified by the chickens. While I was building a fenced yard for them, he would kneel and make cautious clucking sounds at the crated fowl, cringing when they lunged pecking and squawking at the bars of the cage. The kids were amazed to discover that if they looked in the straw-filled boxes in the chicken yard, they would find brown, smooth eggs that they could hold to their cheeks to feel the warmth. Joan and Lisa would follow me out to feed the chickens carrying colorful baskets to gather the eggs. For a while they didn't want us to cook them, in case there were baby chicks inside them, so I had to buy our eggs at the store.

I gave the youngest kids a brief explanation of the life cycle of chickens using a fair amount of creativity, knowing that they'd get more details later when Alice felt that they were old enough. She had sturdy opinions about waiting until they asked more complex questions. She'd waited until the two older girls were each twelve before she'd talked with them about sex.

I admit I was relieved to be let off the hook, but I worried that some day my youngest girls would wonder if I was dishonest or just stupid.

After Clint was born, we knew that five kids would be our limit. I wouldn't have minded another boy, but Alice was clear that this was it. So we focused our attention on raising happy kids in a safe rural setting.

I hurried home from my job teaching high school math every day and set about planting cherry, apple, plum, and dogwood trees. Alice was homesick, and no matter what I did, she seemed depressed. I feared that she would decide to take the kids and move back to Charleston. So I planted two pecan trees in the front yard to help her deal with her distress at living in the "sticks." Alice's mother had three ancient pecan trees in her back garden on Wentworth Street that Alice loved.

By May, after school was out, I felt we'd turned a corner in our new life. Most days we settled into a calm routine and were glad for it. I'd grown up on a farm and hated farm chores, so I joined the Marines for adventure, then met Alice and settled down. Now I discovered that I loved planting a garden and landscaping the yards. I even arranged to have a guy with a bulldozer come over and build a small pond so the kids could fish and play with frogs, as I had as a kid.

Alice and I loved hearing the excitement in the kids' voices with every new discovery. Each day felt a bit like Christmas to me.

Early that summer our middle daughter, Joan, the busy third grader who often thought up mischief, had asked at breakfast if she could buy two rabbits. "I'll use my allowance to feed them," she said. "I can buy two with the money I got for my birthday."

"No," Alice said. "No rabbits." She had answered before we could talk, although we exchanged looks. The kids saw this and sensed a divided front. I knew not to undercut her decisions, but sometimes after we talked privately about something, she'd change her mind or I would change mine. "We're overrun around here with animals. I don't want to be the one having to take care of them. So no."

We didn't know then that Joan had already bought a couple of rabbits from a neighbor's son. Little did we know, even as we were discussing it, the rabbits were huddled in a pen in an old shed behind the garden!

I didn't particularly mind the idea of rabbits, although I remembered from grade school that it didn't take long for a couple of rabbits to multiply in a way that brought new meaning to the term *geometric progression.* But I trusted Alice's instincts about what our kids needed.

We found out we had rabbits the day after this discussion. Lisa, our first grader, had gone outside to feed the new pony a slice of apple, and she ran into the kitchen while we were having breakfast. "We have lots and lots of rabbits." She was jumping up and down. "Come see. Baby bunnies. Everywhere. Tons of them."

The whole family almost trampled me as they raced to the backyard to count ten baby rabbits.

Alice groaned at the wiggling mass of babies and looked at me. "I didn't know," I said. "Honest. I never told Joan yes."

Joan said, "Davy sold me a boy rabbit and a girl rabbit. Please let us keep them." She brought one of the tiny babies to Alice, who stroked its tiny pink face, while the kids marveled that its eyes were sealed shut. "They're blind? Why are they blind? Will they be okay?"

I told her lots of animal babies can't see at first, and that their parents protect them from danger while they are helpless. And then, as I examined the other rabbit, I said, "Well, good news! You don't have a pair. But unfortunately, the other female is going to have babies soon, too."

Alice shook her head and sighed. "Oh, good grief! Okay, I give up, but you all have to help and your father will need to get to work building more pens. When they get old enough, you'll have to find homes for them."

So we let the kids keep the rabbits. How could we say no? I spent the next Saturday afternoon building sturdy hutches with fine wire mesh and runs behind the old tool shed. I added a wire fence and a gate that the kids could open and close by themselves.

A week later the other rabbit gave birth to twelve babies. And a month later, the girls talked me into letting them care for a friend's rabbit while they were away. But Thumper chewed through a wall into a pen that had the first female in it, and after that things got a little out of hand. By August, we had at least thirty rabbits. Although we gave some away, I soon lost count of exactly how many we had.

The kids named them all, and it was quite a sight to see the girls walking around in the backyard followed by a dozen rabbits. They taught some to hop along beside them on a leash. Another one would chase a ball. They played with those bunnies like they were puppies.

But one morning in early August, I looked out the window and saw a pack of dogs circling the chicken yard. I raced out and chased them away. I learned from a neighbor that a family had moved away and left their dogs to roam the neighborhood. Other dogs had joined this ragtag pack. I worried that they might attack the girls and cautioned them to throw rocks at them to scare them away. I considered buying a gun but decided against it with so many kids around.

Later in August, Alice had been especially quiet at dinner one night. After the kids were safely tucked into bed, she told me she was worried that she might be pregnant again. "You promised me this wouldn't happen! I don't have the energy for another child," she said. "I really didn't want a half-dozen children, and I told you that when we married."

I was both happy and sad for us. But what could we do? I vowed to find a way to do more to help. Maybe I could tutor students and get some extra money. Maybe we could get someone to come in and help with the kids. Maybe one of her sisters could come from Charleston for a while when the new baby came. We would find a way.

And I admit that although I adored my beautiful girls, I did hope the new baby would be a boy so Clint could grow up and be someone's big brother.

In September for the long Labor Day weekend, we arranged for one of our neighbors to feed the animals. We piled into the station wagon and drove south to Charleston to see Alice's family. It was our first trip back since we'd moved. Alice had arranged to see her doctor, who confirmed the pregnancy. She was sad and resigned, but we'd decided we would make the best of the situation.

We decided to wait a while before telling the kids about the new baby. We had a good visit, and just before we left to drive home, Alice told her sisters and her mother, who reacted with surprise and sympathy. As I packed the car for our drive home, I really feared that Alice would change her mind and stay in Charleston. So I was relieved when she finally said her good-byes and got into the car.

She cried quietly for a while as we drove home. The kids kept asking me what was wrong. I told them she missed her mommy and sisters. The kids were quiet and I could tell it worried them to see Alice cry like that.

At one point when we stopped at a rest stop, I came back to the car to find them all crying. "We all want to go back to Charleston to live," Joan said. "We don't need rabbits and chickens. Why did you have to make us move?" That four-hour drive seemed to last for days.

Clint was asleep when we got home just before time for dinner. I carried him inside to finish his nap and started to unpack the station wagon. The two older girls went off to see a new friend who lived nearby. The two younger girls, bursting with pent-up energy, leapt out of the car and raced off to see all the animals.

A few minutes later I heard terrible screams, the kind that every parent fears. A scream that tells you something horrible has happened. A scream different from any other sounds you'll ever hear, and even now, remembering it, the hair stands up on the back of my neck. I dropped the suitcase I was carrying into the house and met Alice running down the stairs behind me. "Oh my God. What's happened?"

When Alice and I got to the backyard, both girls were crying hysterically outside the fenced rabbit pens. The torn wire gate lay on the ground beside the cages. Hutches were ripped open; many were upside down with the doors missing and the wire mesh torn and scattered.

Joan held a back leg. Lisa had an ear. Both were screaming and their hands were covered with blood. For a moment, I feared they'd been attacked by whatever had brought such carnage.

I took a step and something crunched beneath my shoe. A white paw. I stood in a killing field and around all those overturned rabbit pens the ground was covered with the remains of rabbits. Tufts of fur blanketed the grass. Tiny puffs of it floated in the air.

Alice knelt and gave me a look of reproach. She held both girls while I walked around the area, trying to make sense of what I was seeing, but how could I make sense of the horrible work of a pack of stray dogs that had been allowed to run loose around the community all summer? Clearly it had happened just before we'd gotten home. Some of the bodies were still warm.

The girls broke away from Alice and we ran from cage to cage, lifting the wrecked doors and looking into the backs of hutches for survivors. They found two. One young doe was so badly injured that she died the moment I lifted her from the ruined cage. Her soft black-and-white fur stuck blood on my hands. The other rabbit, a small white one that Lisa had trained to chase a ball, lay on her side in shock, until I gently slipped my hands under her to examine her.

The minute I lifted her, she emitted a high-pitched tortured sound that made me dizzy with fear. The girls were sobbing and pleading with me to take her to a veterinarian, but that was impossible. The nearest vet was a half-hour drive. As I felt the damage to her underside and warm fluids trickled from her nose and mouth, I knew what I had to do.

I looked back at Alice and said, "Honey, take them to the house and get a shovel." I wanted to cover my ears to stop the awful sound of that poor rabbit, but instead, I slipped my thumb just behind the base of her head along her spine. I whispered, "I'm sorry, I didn't mean for it to be this way," as I pressed as mercifully as I could. She twitched once and went limp in my hands. I felt her heart thrumming a few more feathery strokes through the fur on her chest. Her eyes glazed over and she was quiet. I had never killed anything, not on the farm or as a Marine, and I hope never to again.

My shoulders shook as I stood holding that rabbit; I'm not ashamed to say I cried.

Alice and the girls returned with a shovel. They watched numbly as I set about digging a hole. I looked up when I'd finished. Alice helped our two little girls as they carefully gathered rabbit parts into their egg baskets.

They brought them to me and we buried the rabbits and the baskets near that oak tree at the far end of the garden. The carnage of a pack of wild dogs on a beautiful fall afternoon is hard to explain to children. I'd never prayed over any kind of animal before, but it seemed important to find the right words to do that now.

As I put my arms around Alice and the girls, the sun was going down. The sky was red behind the shed that housed our chickens, left untouched, but addled, by the violent rampage. And I knew there was no safe place.

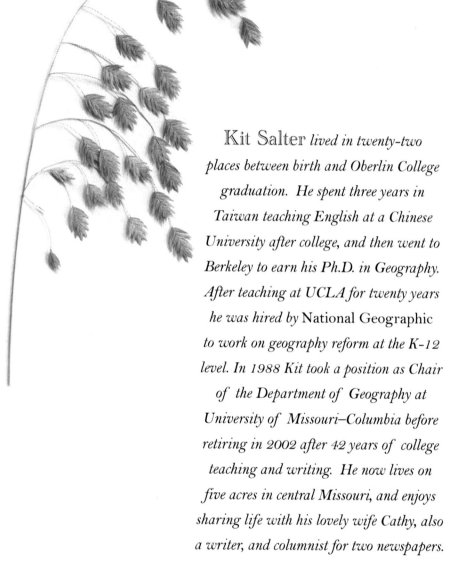

Kit Salter *lived in twenty-two places between birth and Oberlin College graduation. He spent three years in Taiwan teaching English at a Chinese University after college, and then went to Berkeley to earn his Ph.D. in Geography. After teaching at UCLA for twenty years he was hired by* National Geographic *to work on geography reform at the K-12 level. In 1988 Kit took a position as Chair of the Department of Geography at University of Missouri–Columbia before retiring in 2002 after 42 years of college teaching and writing. He now lives on five acres in central Missouri, and enjoys sharing life with his lovely wife Cathy, also a writer, and columnist for two newspapers.*

Memo From the U.S. Bureau of Poetry

Kit Salter

Fiction

In most of the various basements of better-known buildings in Washington, D.C., there exist constellations of so-called 'minor bureaucracies.' They are little known except by those who work there…and those whose lives happen to fall into the realm of their official authority.

For the employees of the specific constellation under study for this narrative, the central node in their professional life is an old maintenance room. As office building needs had grown, the chores necessary to keep the place clean had been outsourced, causing the large room to become newly available as a makeshift basement lounge. It had running water because of the old mop sink. It had ragtag lighting patched together from discarded lamps and not quite dead bulbs. For the initial inhabitants of this room such lighting was good for smoking, quiet conversation, coffee drinking and careful napping. For bureaucratic minions this new setting was a continual twilight zone of governmental inattention. It was outfitted with about a dozen chairs that had been cast away from offices in the building's upper floors.

This haven was casually designated "The Liars Den" by a handmade sign penned with a Sharpie on the back of a recycled manila folder, and was of real moment to the people whose working lives played out in offices down the hall in both directions.

This Liars Den also was the center of semi-official postings of tasks, edicts, and rules promulgated by these same minor bureaucratic centers in the discharge of assigned duties. To anyone entering the Den, the sight of the paper layers mounded on the large drywall bulletin board was so captivating, all who passed paused. Curiosity piqued, they found that careful peeling away of top layers might produce, for example, early directives that prohibited smoking in the offices in 1997 or cautions regarding 1960s Watergate-like threats to basement offices, or even, with extra care and patience, perhaps the handwritten note by General Washington telling of the planned 1776 Christmas Day's crossing of the Delaware River. The potential implication of this mountain of memos was, in fact, enormous.

At the crest of one of the hillocks of memos was a single undated page. It was on formal letterhead from one of the basement Bureaus.

To: All Poets or Potential Poets
Re: Acceptable Language

The U.S. Bureau of Poetry has added the following lines to the inventory of Acceptable Poetic Language and Imagery:

1. "a bleak and desolate winter landscape"
2. "the surly glance of a man too long at the bar"

The Poetry Bureau

3. *"a thin woman, moving like scissors, sliced across the cobbled street"*
4. *"the growing sorrow of a child seemingly forgotten on a lonely beach"*
5. *"winds toying with the trees in nasty abandon"* and
6. *"her astonished response to the presentation of the nearly dead flowers."*
   —**Chairman Ward Smyth**

"What the hell is this?" asked Blake, a long haired man in his forties who had stopped to peruse the ever-growing paper stack on his way into the Den. The query was addressed to the room in general. There were four others present when he voiced his question.

Across the room, Stanley said, with some uncertainty in his voice, "I'm pretty sure that's the latest document created by our new **Bureau of Poetry** in Room B-157."

"Yeah," responded Blake before Stanley could go any farther in his speculation. "I see it's got a local look, but what's it mean? I can't imagine that we've actually created a Bureau of Poetry." Blake—who worked in the **Bureau of Superfluous Redundancies**—spoke in a tone that was a blend of disbelief and frustration. He went on before a response came his way. "We can't even find enough frigging money to get regular key cards installed here and yet some whiz talks the **Bureau of Bureaucracies** into regulating poetry! How the hell can this be?"

The two women in the Den let their conversation drop. The other man in the room put down the report he was reading to attend to the developing discussion.

Brenda, a tall redhead who worked in the **Bureau of Incidental Music in Commercial Spaces** walked over to the wallpaper of past memos and read the six 'acceptable' images. She spoke with more authority than had been mustered by Stanley. "I'm certain this has been done to supposedly streamline America's creative energies. Some months ago there was a lament posted here from the **Bureau of Intelligent Use of Our National Intelligence.** It claimed that 'Intellectuals waste too much time on pointless argumentation over subjective poetry and fiction.' That memo noted that a sub-committee had been assigned to streamline poetic thinking. My guess is that sub-committee morphed into this new **Bureau of Poetry.**"

"Poetic thinking?" questioned Martha, who worked in the office of **The Bureau of Regulation of Parking Meter Height and Bicycle Locks.** She looked too bright to have others fully discount her views. "There's no such thing as poetic thinking, Brenda." There was a strident quality in Martha's words. "Poetry is almost always a nearly random collection of whimsy words. Word choice is probably guided by typos authors make forcing them to search out words that would accommodate their digital ineptitude. This process was surely initiated when early typewriters allowed no correction of mistyped words except through really troublesome Wite-Out."

"Who cares whether or not poetry is whimsy?" asked Stanley, coming forward and growing into his presentation. "The government doesn't pay a cent for it. Our cities are filled with countless nervous intellectuals who believe that if they can write or publish or critique bundles of words called 'poetry,' they will gain merit in their precious circles of unemployed and nervous artisans." To all in the room these words came as a surprise. Stanley was the classic fence sitter on most issues raised in The Liars Den. He was the oldest of the employees in the room, and spoke with the authority that he hoped his suit and vest implied. He worked in the **Bureau of Highway Pothole Fulfillment.**

"You're right about the people, but you're wrong about the costs, Stanley," responded Clyde. "We're all paying for a lack of guidance all the time." He stood up from the table where he had been sitting alone and walked toward the memo board while continuing his remarks, "All the damned governmental regulations designed to open every door to everyone for every crazy thing mean that we've become a society without any clarified performance standards." He paused by the board and then went on. "The fact that we now have a **U.S. Bureau of Poetry** might possibly mean we will no longer need the government to continue to pay for the annual publication of *The Newsletter of Children Who Have Had Their Lunch Money Stolen*— just to cite one example."

Clyde, an employee of the **Bureau of Requested but Unclaimed Library Books,** turned to the directive in question saying, "Look at this first image... *'a bleak and desolate winter landscape.'* That's a great line for images of what climate change is doing to us. Such a theme and image would not only bring poetry into focus, but it could be used in education to jumpstart children or young adults into thinking about something really important like greenhouse gases obscuring life-giving sunlight...instead of who's got the baddest Nikes in the classroom."

Clearly stimulated by his own surprise at the lack of argumentation, he pushed on. "Or, think of all that can be linked to this poetic line *'the growing sorrow of a child seemingly forgotten on a lonely beach.'* That image just cries out for parents to come back to real parenting for their very real children!" He turned a little bit so that he could present his face of genuine, even daring, conviction to the rest of the basement dwellers in The Liars Den. It appeared that Stanley had now gained an ally in Clyde. Alliances were always fluid among the basement bureaucrats.

"Oh, horse pucky, Clyde," protested Martha, on break from **Parking Meters and Bicycle Locks.** "Poetry's not written to show what should be done. It's meant to illustrate what has been done by or to the poet, the author. Maybe there's some language given to exhortations for future action, but the real message of the poet is 'Look at me. Look what I have been through. Feel for me.'"

Uncertain Promise 149

Martha paused just for a second to let people ponder her pronouncement. Then she went on. "Making such writers adhere to basement guidelines created in our windowless world is not going change the flow of poetic self-pity or self-promotion." She, too, was now moving toward the directive on the well-papered wall.

The redhead turned toward Martha. "What's your idea of a poem, Martha?" asked Brenda. "Something graceful like 'Close cover before striking?' That's the most published line in the history of the English language and it doesn't say a thing about the past. It is entirely focused on future action—but then again, you're probably too young to ever have seen matchbooks with this universal exhortation."

"And, Stanley, " added Blake, eager to keep the tone of the group suspicious about the memo, "since you seem to have been charting the progress of our new Bureau of basement Poetry, what's your definition of poetry?" He rushed on before Stanley could reply. "How about this, Stan? 'Candy is dandy but liquor is quicker.'"

Stanley's chance to respond was interrupted—to his apparent relief—by Brenda. "Oh, swell, Blake, give us that classic Ogden Nash couplet. He's called a poet, but he really should be labeled more a…a master teacher. In putting liquor ahead of candy in winning access to a woman's heart---or other body zones---he's acting like a tour guide. He's saying—and he's using poetic rhyme as a come-on---'I've tried many ploys to gain access and I can tell you that liquor is the most effective tool as a way finder.'" She then quickly added---after a nanosecond of consideration-- "Nash might have said 'Flowers are power---and whiskeys are sour—but a sweet splash of Jack puts the gal on her back,' but poetic circles would be alarmed at such crassness." The redhead studied the shocked looks on the faces of her fellow minions and concluded with a grin, saying, "The poetic muse needs camouflage. Every tour guide knows there has to be some mystery in exploration and discovery."

The Poetry Bureau

In a moment of silence various postures were considered in this brand new Liars Den dialogue. Stanley, the suited man, spoke first—carefully dodging comment on all that Brenda had posited. "I found myself captured by the line—I think it was Acceptable Image 2—*'the surly glance of a man too long at the bar.'* The whole package of images that weave around drink, bars, surly--and often lonely--men...all of these things can be the very bedrock of vital outreach that is both social and governmental. We all know bureaucrats have a difficult time really solving problems but this directive does show a potentially guiding light on problems that run through our whole society."

"What are you saying, Stan?" asked Blake, with incredulity in his voice. "Have you bought into the zingy concept that these restrictions have some possible merit? Have you really thought about this or is this just another effort to be a carbon copy of the people upstairs in hope for ascension?" Though the question was asked by Blake, all of them had long wondered why Stanley came to work daily in a suit, although not always with a vest, while the rest of them came in a permanent 'Friday Casual' mode.

Stanley stared squarely at Blake, speaking with more force than was customary for the suited man. "Blake, why not free your narrow mind from whining for a minute and think of these words, this image: *'a thin woman, moving like scissors, sliced across the cobbled street.'* Can't you emerge from the depression you seem always to feel because of your work in the **Bureau of Superfluous Redundancies?** Why not open your mind and consider the beauty of that scene...the woman, her legs, her pace, the cobbled street surface? That's what this memo is calling for...the recognition of these lines as being central to true poetic imagery and writing—and maybe even new thinking."

A wide grin crept across Blake's face. "Wow...Stanley. A real feeling. A genuine utterance of mini-protest. A declaration of a sensation that almost trumps your vest!" Blake looked around the room, expecting a chorus of support, at least in laughter, if not in affirming comments.

Instead he heard, "And what about *'winds toying with the trees in nasty abandon?'*" This question came from Clyde, who had walked closer to the memo to be able to quote acceptable image # 5 verbatim. "There's real power in sensing that nature itself is at play here, not just the forces of indifferent humankind and its destruction of the earth."

Blake and Martha looked at each other. The alignment of the Den now seemed to have Stanley, Brenda and even Clyde representing an alliance between **Highway Pothole Fulfillment, Parking Meter Height and Bicycle Locks** and **Unclaimed Library Books**.

Martha broke the momentary silence. "No poets will allow themselves to be constrained by bureaucratic rules about so-called 'acceptable language.'"

"You're wrong, Martha," claimed Brenda, with Stanley quick to nod his head in agreement. "Poets have no Body Politic. They all either live in isolated garrets or they make little corners in dark coffee houses and while away their ill-spent time scribbling in partially used notebooks with Number 2 pencils. The only thing that brings them together is frequent attendance at local art gallery wine receptions for new shows. They can find a full meal free even at these most minimal grazing tables."

Before anyone could respond, Stanley added, "If they had any real purpose in their lives, they'd try to find a job in useful agencies like some of the ones we work for." He beamed proudly at being able to return the discussion to things local and to the realities of salaried employment.

The others all looked at each other with a mixture of grimace and grin. Such facial dexterity was a vital trait of all who worked as minions in the underground bureaucracies of this building.

Blake spoke. "Stanley, Martha, Clyde--you're right on. You've got it figured out. Poets will live by the Agreeable Language Directive because they don't have the gumption to find meaningful work such as we have. Or, better yet, if they want truly to be successful, they'll write poems that use one or more of this Memo's six Acceptable Images as foundation themes. They could be published as short governmental reports. I can see the new pubs now: 'Desolate Landscapes as Tutors for the Green Future,' or 'Reasons for Not Toying with Trees in Abandon,' or 'Surly Men Turned Resource Managers Though Poetry.'"

"It won't be as simple..." began Brenda.

Martha interrupted her. "Not so, Brenda. You three have found a truly simple approach to all of these issues. Even though I'm not a believer in anything poetic, I suggest that your combined reactions might be expressed through something like this 'poetry.'

'No Poetry; No Problem.

Know Poetry. Know too many Problems.

No better way to hide the problems than

To control the language.'

"How does that seem to the three of you?"

By this time, people were headed toward the door to return to their various desks. Stanley walked over to Martha and took her by the arm. "Martha, Clyde...we have to go." Then, as soon as the three of them were a little bit separated from Brenda and Blake in the windowless corridor, he said, "I've got a meeting with the Chief of the **Bureau of Poetry** in a few minutes. He says he has five new phrases that he thinks might be acceptable poetic images. Do you two have time to come and review them with me?"

As they all left, the weak light of the Liars Den seemed to be just perfect for that space.

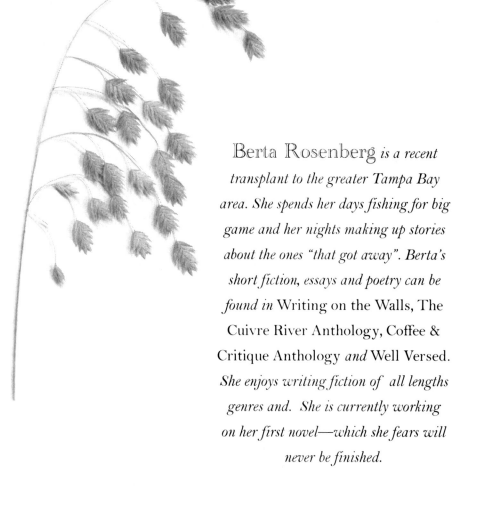

Berta Rosenberg *is a recent transplant to the greater Tampa Bay area. She spends her days fishing for big game and her nights making up stories about the ones "that got away". Berta's short fiction, essays and poetry can be found in* Writing on the Walls, The Cuivre River Anthology, Coffee & Critique Anthology *and* Well Versed. *She enjoys writing fiction of all lengths genres and. She is currently working on her first novel—which she fears will never be finished.*

A Blessing

Berta Rosenberg

Fiction

To stop the banging from the other side, I yanked the door open and caught her mid-pound. Her swollen belly led the way as she toppled across the threshold. The third trimester bulge was the only thing about her that was large. I wondered for a second where she found maternity clothes small enough to fit her tiny frame. Reaching out with both hands, I steadied her. She smelled of cigarettes.

"Lyndzy, what a surprise," I forced a smile.

"I can't do this, Marilyn." She was on the brink of crying.

"Come on, I'll make us some tea."

In the kitchen she put her head on the table and sobbed. I took my time with the tea, steeling myself for a rough afternoon. Just like old times—all Lyndzy, all the time. How many years had it been since she burst into our lives with those sweet brown eyes and that little-girl smile hiding a mountain of heartache floating in a river of tears?

Without bothering to ask if she was hungry, I made a sandwich and slid it in front of her, then grabbed the tissues and brought them to the table with the tea. I sat down across from her, and she immediately reached for me. I let her take my hand. After only three months, I wasn't even close to being cried out myself. Digging deep, I searched for the compassion to comfort the little urchin.

"What was I thinking? I can't raise this baby by myself," she gasped between sobs.

"I know. It's going to be hard," was all I could manage.

For the past four years, the idea of a grandbaby from this child had been my fiercest nightmare. When Jeremy turned sixteen, I bought a box of condoms and put them in his underwear drawer. Call me crazy, but I made sure he had an unlimited supply. I tried to talk to him about her and reason with him. But he would never see it. In his eyes, she was perfect.

She mopped her tears and snot with a paper napkin and bit into the sandwich. "My mom kicked me out again," she said, her mouth still full.

I have to admit—Lyndzy never had a fair shot. Over the years, I had called her mother, Sharon, many things. Mentally stable is not on that list. I think somehow, even when they were small children, Jeremy knew the table was tilted away from Lyndzy. Maybe it even drew him to her. From rescuing strays to defending bullied kids at school, he could never resist a lost cause.

During their sophomore year, he started spending more and more time with Lyndzy. They became a couple. Things weren't all bad at first. She was around our house more than when they were kids. The two grew inseparable. Gradually his other friends

A Blessing

dropped away. Later, when pressed, one of them said they just couldn't take Lyndzy anymore. They hated seeing her drag him around by the ring she had in his nose.

The two of them would cruise along for a while. But, ultimately, he would do something to upset her and she would break up with him. The roller coaster never idled long. They had fights, not just arguments or lovers' quarrels. They fought. Twice I took him to the hospital for stitches after he put his hand through a window or a wall during a fight. Once he was treated for a broken wrist after defending her honor with some boy she claimed touched her inappropriately.

Moody became the new normal. He lost interest in the things he enjoyed. His grades suffered. He quit the swim team. Correction – I thought he quit the swim team. I later found out he was kicked off; I still don't know why. He started missing curfew. Sometimes he didn't come home at all. He and Joe fought, and more than once, they came to physical blows.

Occasionally, we caught glimpses of our sweet Jeremy, but ultimately, something would go wrong between him and Lyndzy and the pot would boil over again. In the end, our once honor-roll son barely met the requirements to receive his high school diploma and graduated a semester late.

Lyndzy blew on her tea and looked at me from behind the cup. I braced myself for the words I knew would follow.

"Marilyn, I know we haven't always agreed on things. I know I wouldn't have been your first choice for Jeremy. But, well, I was sort of hoping. . ." She nervously twisted the dainty engagement ring on her bony finger.

I looked away, eager to deny the role I played in the disintegration of my family. Five months had past and still I struggled with my actions on the night of their engagement.

Our last Christmas Eve had started out with just enough snow for a white Christmas, but not enough to muck up the roads and cause problems. Joe took two weeks' vacation and, for once, we had enough time to decorate every inch of the house, inside and out. We hung handmade wreaths on the doors and windows, strung popcorn for the tree and draped garland on the banister. Joe and I cooked enough food to feed the entire town and invited everyone we knew for a holiday open house. The smell of glazed ham and freshly baked biscuits filled the air. We had major cause for celebration: Jeremy was home from Marine Corps boot camp and was finally getting his life back on track.

Jeremy was his old outgoing self as he mingled with the relatives and neighbors. Always such a handsome boy, in his dress uniform he outshone even the sparkle of the freshly cut Douglas fir. Lyndzy was right there, hanging onto Jeremy lest he disappear should she happen to let go.

Sharon dropped by. Apparently having had a few drinks elsewhere, she was her usual boisterous self. She flirted first with one neighbor and then others, quickly moving on to the next as each wife in turn reclaimed their territory.

As the party wound down, with only Sharon, Lyndzy, a few close friends and relatives still in the house, Jeremy asked for everyone's attention.

"Lyndzy and I are getting married. We're gonna be parents." He stood proudly in the center of the room, Lyndzy looked like a child next to him, his arm wrapped protectively around her shoulders. He held up her left hand for everyone to see the engagement ring perched there. The tiny diamond glistened, reflecting the twinkling lights of the tree.

Before I could react, Sharon staggered over and grabbed me in a gin-shrouded bear hug. "Marilyn, we're gonna be grammas together," she slurred, losing her balance and pulling us both down on the sofa. "Can you imagine? Me, a grandma." She batted her eyelashes at Joe.

I sat stunned, trying to keep the tears at bay. As quickly as I could, I excused myself to the kitchen and began putting food away and loading the dishwasher. I knew I had to hold it together until I could talk with Jeremy privately.

A few minutes later I heard Sharon looking for me to say goodnight. I snuck out the back door and hid in the garage, peeking out the window, until I saw Jeremy walking Sharon and Lyndzy home.

"Aw, crap," was all Joe said after we bid goodbye to the remaining guests and resumed clean up duty. He never was one to carry on about such things.

"Are you going to talk to him?" I asked.

"He's a grown man. What's left to say?"

I heard Jeremy come back inside, he stomped snow off his shoes and started gathering the half-empty glasses and dirty plates from the living room. I poured the last of the eggnog punch into a cup and added an accessory splash of bourbon. "Let's sit a minute," I said as he entered the kitchen.

"Have you thought about what you're going to do?" I collapsed into a chair.

"What do you mean, what I'm gonna do? I have to report back for duty in three weeks. That's what I'm gonna do."

"You know that's not what I'm talking about." I lowered my voice, but didn't look away.

He stared at me in silent reply.

"I mean the pregnancy," I said.

"You mean the baby?" he corrected me.

"I suppose that is what I meant. You know, you have other options."

Berta Rosenberg

"Wow. This is beyond even you, Mother. I know you've never liked Lyndzy, but to suggest. . . Well, help me out here. Exactly what are you suggesting?"

"I just don't want you to ruin your life." The words propelled themselves from my throat. I snapped my mouth shut in an attempt to keep further syllables from escaping.

"So, to avoid ruining my life, you would suggest I murder your grandchild?"

It was my turn for silence.

"You and Lyndzy have more in common than you think. That was her first impulse, too."

"You know, your father and I only want what's best for you." Again, the words—I was incapable of restraining them.

"Sharon's right. You're a self-righteous bitch," he nodded, agreeing with himself.

He slammed the kitchen door as he left.

That was the last time we saw him. A few days later I returned from the grocery store and found his house key on the kitchen counter. A quick check of his room revealed the few things he had brought from boot camp were gone. I phoned him daily during the remaining weeks of his leave, but he wouldn't answer and never returned my calls. He refused to see me when I drove to Sharon's and ignored my attempts to apologize.

On a cold Sunday in February, it was snowing again when the doorbell rang. It was only three o'clock, but dark clouds ruled the angry afternoon sky. The flakes were sticky and wet. The two uniformed men on our porch were somber and uncomfortable looking. I put my back to the unopened door and slid to the floor. I called for Joe, my cry piercing the quiet afternoon, shattering our world. I sat there holding my breath. Silent tears slipped down my face.

A Blessing

Joe pulled me to my feet before opening the door and ushering the men inside. They entered in slow motion, stamping their feet to remove the snow, exactly as Jeremy had the last time he came through that door. They placed their caps under their arms and stood shoulder to shoulder. I didn't hear a word. There was no need to listen. Their presence said it all.

It could have happened anywhere. That sunny California morning Jeremy left Camp Pendleton to run errands. A speeding SUV ran a stoplight and broadsided his compact car. Jeremy was killed on impact.

Joe and I struggled through the next days and weeks. Months. Lyndzy wouldn't speak to us at the service. In the funeral home, we sat on opposing sides of the room as if in court, each contemplating an unspoken indictment of the other.

We offered help with the baby, financial and otherwise. At first, she rebuffed our efforts, explaining Jeremy would not have wanted us—me—involved with the baby. After the first ultrasound, which she attended alone because Sharon forgot, she softened a bit. She brought us a grainy image. Our grandson in profile. Soon, she started dropping by once in a while, gave us updates, let us feel the baby kick. She planned to name him Jeremy.

She set her cup down a little too hard. "Marilyn I want you to adopt the baby open closed whatever it takes I want you and Joe to raise him," she said it all in one burst, no pauses, as if she were afraid the words would die in her throat if she took time for a breath.

My heart swelled. I resisted the urge to hug her. I knew the request was coming. What I hadn't known was the struggle it would bring. Which misery do I choose?

Joe and I had talked about this. We figured it was only a matter of time before she asked. How great was the temptation to think that would be the end of it? That she would hand over our grandson and quietly exit, stage left? No, we would be tied to this woman-child for the rest of our lives.

I sipped my tea and shook my head. "No, Lyndzy. We'll help you however you need, but we can't take the baby. It'll be hard, but you can do it."

She started bawling again. "I don't have a job. I don't even have a place to live."

"You can stay here. We'll set up the guest room for you. The baby can have Jeremy's old room." A lone tear slid down my face, challenging my resolve.

"I couldn't do that."

"Not forever, just 'til you get your life straightened out."

"Don't you have to talk to Joe?"

"What's there to talk about? We'll go pick up your things when he gets home."

Lyndzy tried, unsuccessfully, to squelch a yawn.

"You look wiped out. How 'bout a nap?" I rinsed our cups and put the milk away.

"Can I take it in Jeremy's room? Just this once." New tears filled her eyes, but they stayed put, did not flood her face.

Quietly, I led the way to Jeremy's room. Over the past months, I had been in there a few times. I dusted. I vacuumed. For hours I sat and wept. More than once, I cried myself to sleep on his bed, clutching his pillow. At first, the linens had still smelled of his shower gel. I got Lyndzy a light blanket from the closet and helped her get comfortable.

I closed the door behind me and said a little prayer for Lyndzy and my grandson. Selfishly, I added another for myself. I may never comprehend the love my son had for this girl, but I would treasure it. I would comfort her, protect her, try to guide her and,

A Blessing

if she allowed, help her raise my baby's son. In the end, I could only hope that this time I had chosen the lesser of the heartbreaks laid upon my table.

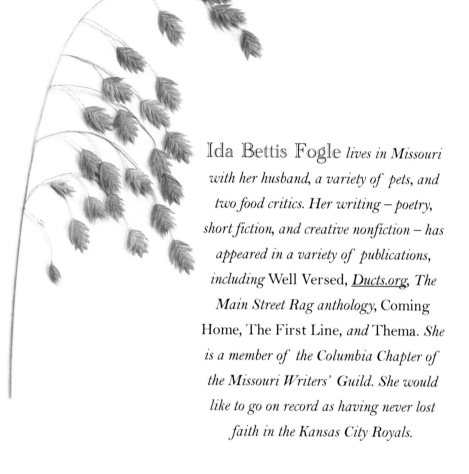

Ida Bettis Fogle *lives in Missouri with her husband, a variety of pets, and two food critics. Her writing – poetry, short fiction, and creative nonfiction – has appeared in a variety of publications, including* Well Versed, Ducts.org, The Main Street Rag *anthology,* Coming Home, The First Line, *and* Thema. *She is a member of the Columbia Chapter of the Missouri Writers' Guild. She would like to go on record as having never lost faith in the Kansas City Royals.*

Some Kind of Royalty

Ida Bettis Fogle

Fiction

I rubbed my hands together under the air dryer until every last drop of moisture evaporated. I was putting off the decision waiting for me right outside the door of the ladies' room: what to do about the bones.

I'd seen them on my way into the restroom, a stack of rawhide chews for dogs, on a shelf at the back of the convenience store. I wished I hadn't noticed them. Then I wouldn't be faced with making a conscious choice about whether to get one for my dad's mutt. Mutt probably wasn't the right word; the thing was half beagle, as my father liked to point out. As I held out my hands, I caught sight of my watch and realized I was on the verge of being late to my dad's birthday dinner.

Right. I pushed open the door with purpose and strode straight to the shelf with the bones, selecting the largest one, telling myself

I was mature enough not to be jealous of a canine. I took three steps, then turned around and put it back on the shelf. I went to the coffee station, filled two cups and started toward the register. Halfway there, I turned and went back for the bone.

Once in the parking lot, I threw the thing into the back seat of my car, next to my dad's gift. Then I phoned my brother, getting his voice mail.

"Chuck, this is April," I said. "I'm five minutes from your place. I hope you're ready."

He wasn't ready. The sound of his phone had awakened him and he'd managed to get mostly dressed before I arrived, but he still needed to put on his shoes and brush his teeth.

As we got into the car, he said, "I need to get some coffee."

I pointed to the cup holder. "I brought you some."

He blinked several times. "Oh, thanks."

Neither of us said anything else until the St. Louis Arch came into view. Chuck motioned toward it. "We gotta kidnap Mom some time and take her up there. Whenever one of us went there on a school field trip, she'd say she was going to get around to seeing it from the inside some day, too. But I don't think she ever did before her and dad moved away." He craned his neck to look into my back seat. "Your car's kind of small, but I think we could fit her in."

I shot him a look and he started backpedaling. "Um, I mean it's nice, your car, and environmentally responsible, and I really appreciate you giving me a ride since my truck's in the shop, and... is that enough? Did I say the right things? Can I stop?"

"Close enough."

"Here, while I'm on a good-brother roll, let me give you my part of the money for Dad's birthday present." He dug some cash out of his pocket and put it into my glove box. "What are we giving him, by the way?"

"Muck boots."

"What?"

Some Kind of Royalty

"You know, those big rubber boots you wear for tromping around in the mud. I figure he can use them when he takes that dog of his –"

"Prince," Chuck supplied.

"Yeah, him," I continued "When they go out hunting squirrels or whatever it is they do out in the woods, Dad can use these muck boots and then take them off by the door, so he doesn't have to worry about getting the floor muddy when he comes in."

"So they're really for Mom, then?"

"I suppose."

"April?"

"Hmmm?"

"If you hate Dad's dog so much, what's with the bone back there?"

"I'm trying to make peace with having it in the family. Besides, I don't hate the thing."

"Prince."

"Yeah that one. I'm happy to see Dad softening up, finding out he's capable of showing affection for...something."

"You think if we'd been as adoring and obedient as a beagle, Dad would have paid us more attention?"

"Isn't it only half beagle?"

"You mean Prince?" Chuck was deliberately needling me.

"Yes, Prince. He gets treated like some kind of royalty, doesn't he? With his little bed by dad's desk. Dad always made us stay out of his office when he was doing paperwork. And he never leaves the house without calling the dog. *Come on Prince, let's go for a drive. Come on Prince, let's go hunting. Come on Prince, let's go see what the squirrels are up to.* He never took either of us along anywhere."

"I know. One day he'd tell us we couldn't do his errands with him because he'd be gone too long and we'd get bored. The next he'd say he would be back home before we knew it anyway so what was the point in us bothering to get ready and in the car."

"He could never be bothered at all, even for the big things."

"Like when I had my appendix out," Chuck said. "I remember waking up after the surgery. Mom was there, but dad had gone home."

"He never came to my band concerts, either," I added. "Or even my grade school graduation."

"He didn't come to my high school graduation," Chuck said. We were one-upping each other now.

"You didn't graduate," I reminded him.

"Okay then, he didn't come with me when I picked up my GED certificate. You think he'll actually wear those boots?"

"I got them in camouflage colors, so he could feel manly about it." I paused, then added. "Maybe if he doesn't like them, he'll at least like that I got something for Prince. You think it might redeem me with him a little, after my big failures in the staying married and producing children departments?"

Chuck snorted. "You're not the failure in the family, April. You're a big-shot engineer. I'm the one making a piecemeal living as a handyman."

"Yeah, but I'm a girl—"

"Whatever." This was Chuck's way of shutting me down before I could get my feminist rant on.

I changed the subject. "Look. There's the Quilt Barn." We were well outside the suburbs now. I always considered myself officially in the country when I saw this landmark, a barn with quilts hanging on every side. The quilts were different every time I drove past. "It's kind of nice to get out of the city sometimes isn't it?"

"Yeah, it's all bucolic and stuff. Sure doesn't smell like coffee houses any more, either," my brother said, putting his hand over his nose. Then, with a look of dismay on his face, he reached for the sun visor. Pulling it down he examined his reflection in the attached mirror. "I do look as stubbly as I feel. Guess I should've

Some Kind of Royalty

shaved; looks like I'm in for a lecture about personal hygiene as relates to career prospects. Hey, you think you could stop at a Casey's or something so I can buy razors?"

"We're already running late, after you oversleeping," I told him. "Mom'll have dinner waiting for us. I'm not standing around in a convenience store waiting for you to shave in their bathroom."

"Just let me run in and get some razors then. I can knock back the stubble in the car on the way, as long as you don't drive too crazy."

"And get whiskers all over my upholstery? Not likely."

"Fine. If Dad says anything, I'll tell him you told me not to take time to shave."

"Whatever."

Chuck busied himself fiddling with my satellite radio. That kept him busy for quite a while. Eventually he looked up, reading a road sign: "Weaverton, 8. Is that the distance or the population?"

"Both," I answered.

In fact, the population was around 900. My parents lived outside of town in a one-level ranch with a small amount of acreage. My dad had bought the place on a whim shortly after his retirement, and had spent the three intervening years trying to put a good face on his decision. He'd stocked up on expensive motorized toys he called tools – a wood chipper, for instance. I don't think he ever used it; the important thing to him was having it. I theorized Prince was part of the image he was trying to cultivate, whatever that might be. If Dad was doing country, he was going to do it in the way he thought looked right, with not just any dog but a beagle, or at least half-beagle.

"And here's the manor," Chuck announced as I pulled into the long gravel drive.

As we neared the house, I heard a dog bark. It came running from behind the house, keeping pace with my Prius as I slowed to a stop. When I opened the door, I realized it was a strange dog, not Prince, though it did look similar. This one was smaller, not completely grown. Its tail was wagging, so I decided I could safely exit the car. My dad appeared from the same direction the dog had.

"Finally here?" he said by way of greeting.

"Yeah, sorry we're a little late," I said. Damn! I hadn't been going to apologize.

"Happy birthday Dad," Chuck said. "We brought you a present."

"Okay, bring it in. We'll see you in the house," Then, addressing the dog, he patted his leg, saying, "Let's go."

He headed inside, the new pet trotting at his heels.

Once the door closed, I turned to Chuck. "Another dog? How many does he need?"

Chuck shrugged. "Can you have too much adoration? Maybe he discovered he really loves dogs."

I opened the back car door to retrieve Dad's gift and eyed the single rawhide bone. Two dogs now. What to do? I stashed the bone under the seat, out of sight.

Chuck and I entered the house to find our father already seated, while my mother put the last of the dinner on the table. "Perfect timing," she said as she saw us. "I just got everything ready."

We both kissed her, and then took our places at the table. I handed the package to my dad. "Happy birthday!" I said.

He removed the giftwrap, handing it to my mom. Then he opened the box and eyed the boots for a minute before saying, "Thanks. Hope they fit."

He started to place the box on the floor next to his chair, but the new dog was there. Dad looked at my mom for a minute before she finally conceded to take the hint. She took the box from him. "Aren't those nice?" she said. "Something you can really use. Thank you kids."

She disappeared into their bedroom, returning a minute later, empty-handed. "Go ahead and dig in," she said to me. Dad and Chuck hadn't waited for her return to start filling their plates.

Some Kind of Royalty

I saw my father eyeing Chuck's stubbly chin.

"Are these tomatoes from your garden?" I asked pre-emptively.

"I picked them this morning," my mom replied.

"They're great, better than anything you get at the grocery store."

"That's one benefit of retiring here," she said. "We have a good garden spot and time to do something with it."

"When she's not reading," my dad added.

My mom put on a taut smile. "That's another thing I finally have time for."

There was nothing to do in Weaverton. Really. Nothing. But my mom was making the best of it, as she always seemed to do.

"I need to thank you again for helping us get our Internet set up here. I didn't know what I was going to do here without a library or bookstore of any kind. But now I know all of the places on the computer where you can buy books."

"Sometimes I walk through the door there," my dad gestured toward the living room, "and I don't know if it's a house or a bookstore. The UPS driver knows where we live now, that's for sure." He pointed his fork toward my plate. "You might want to think about your portions there, April."

So he'd noticed my new eight pounds. In my mind I wanted to rebel by shoveling in what I had and taking seconds. But my stomach felt as if it were shrinking. I had trouble forcing down anything. As I pushed the roast beef and mashed potatoes around my plate, I noticed my dad slipping bits of meat to the dog. I realized I had been waiting for Prince to show up and wondered where he was.

Chuck must have been on the same train of thought because he asked out loud. "Where's Prince?"

My mom cleared her throat and shot an angry glance at my dad, who hesitated a split second before answering in a tone that sounded as if he intended to placate someone. "Aww, he's got a new home." He then gestured to the new dog and his voice shifted to boasting mode. "This boy here is a *full-blooded* beagle. Best hunting dogs around. A guy over in Cedar Grove breeds them." He reached down to pat the dog on the head, saying, "You don't miss a critter in the woods, do you boy?"

"So...what? You just got rid of Prince? Just gave him away?" I blurted out.

"He'll be fine. No need for you to get all worked up. I didn't think you were too fond of him anyway. Don't know why you're upset he's gone." Dad answered.

"He worshiped you, Dad. He loved you with all his heart and you threw him out like an old shoe." My voice rose in pitch as I went on.

"Prince loves everyone he meets. He'll get along anywhere," my father said.

I felt a sudden surge of kinship with the little not-quite-whole-beagle and found myself hoping he'd at least gone to someone kind. Perhaps a family with children who would take care of him into his old age. "Who has him now?"

My father gave my mother a look that told me this point had been an issue between them. Then he said, looking at no one in particular. "A friendly dog like him, I'm sure all sorts of people would want him. He's got to be in a great home by now."

Chuck's eyebrows worked their way toward the ceiling. He said, "So you...like...took him to a shelter or something?"

"You didn't," I said.

"That place they have over in Cedar Grove is downright posh," my dad sounded defensive now. "Those animals live better than some people. And like I said, Prince probably didn't stay there more than a day before someone decided to take him."

"Probably?" I asked. "Probably? Did you call to find out? Have you even checked to see what happened to him?"

"Don't need to. I know someone will take him. Probably already have."

Some Kind of Royalty

The new dog stood up, made his way to Chuck's feet and started sniffing his shoes. That happened a lot with Chuck and dogs. Chuck looked down at him and asked, "What's this one's name?"

"King," my father answered.

For a moment, I imagined myself back at a junior high band performance, putting a flute to my mouth and scanning the crowd for my missing dad, wondering if he would have attended had I made first chair. I bolted from my seat at the dinner table. "I'm leaving," I announced, while striding to the door.

Chuck looked startled. "Should I come?"

"If you don't want to hitchhike."

He shoveled in one last large bite of food before following me. Mom was right there behind him, saying, "Kids, don't leave so soon." But I didn't stop.

Mom followed us out to the car. As I reached for the door handle, she grabbed my arm. "Can't we have one meal together without something like this?"

"After what he did?"

"You always find something to fight with him about."

"*I* always find something? He always does something, and you never stop him."

I pulled my arm away, but my mom positioned herself between me and the car. "That's not fair. I don't like it any more than you do. But you have to understand what your dad's been through in life. He grew up with almost nothing. What little he did have was always the cheapest, worst quality, and usually second or third hand..."

"I don't care. You should have stopped him, anyway."

I looked to Chuck for support, but he stood looking at the ground, staying out of it.

"He didn't tell me what he was doing," my mom said. "He left with Prince and I thought they were just going for a drive. Then he came back with the other one. I tried to get him to change his mind, but he wouldn't."

I turned again to Chuck. "Get in."

I opened my door and started to sit, but caught sight of my mom's face, specifically the tears in her eyes. I never could stay mad at her, no matter how much I wanted to. I gave her a hug. "I can't stay."

As I pulled out of the drive, Chuck said, "Um, April?"

"Yeah?"

"You're heading the wrong direction."

"No, I'm not."

"Okay. Where are we going?"

"Cedar Grove. To the animal shelter."

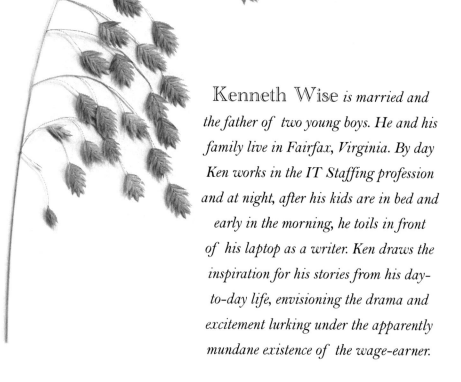

Kenneth Wise *is married and the father of two young boys. He and his family live in Fairfax, Virginia. By day Ken works in the IT Staffing profession and at night, after his kids are in bed and early in the morning, he toils in front of his laptop as a writer. Ken draws the inspiration for his stories from his day-to-day life, envisioning the drama and excitement lurking under the apparently mundane existence of the wage-earner.*

Sledding

Kenneth Wise

Fiction

Ring
Ring
"Hello?" I hear silence then heavy breathing. "I know who this is and why you are calling," The person on the other end hangs up. A few seconds later, the phone rings again. Once again heavy breathing. "Hello?" I say.
After a few seconds, a voice talking louder than it should says, "Daddy, when are you going to be home? If you don't hurry up, we won't be able to go."
"I'm almost in the neighborhood." I turn the corner, flatten a lump of snow, feel the car fishtail a bit, straighten out and pull onto our street. "Put all of your snow clothes on. I'll change real quick, and we'll go."
"I already have everything on. I just need to find my boots."

"Ask Mom where they are. She knows where everything is."

The phone goes quiet for a moment and another voice comes on. "Kevin, after you get home, you're going to need to shovel the driveway, check the gutters, and straighten up the house."

"I thought we just cleaned it."

"I know, but my mother is coming, and this place gets so messy so fast."

I switch the phone to my other ear, hold it in place between my chin and shoulder and reach over to turn the radio down. "Wasn't she just here two weeks ago?"

"Jenny invited mom to come and see her kids in the Christmas pageant, so she is going to stay here for the week."

"Why doesn't she just stay at Jenny's house?"

"We've had this conversation a million times. Mom feels more comfortable here."

"I'm glad someone does," I say.

"Do you want to have a discussion about this again?"

"I know it won't do any good. Anyway, I'm almost there. I'll be inside in a second." I hang up.

As I approach the house, I hit the gas to gain enough momentum to go up the steep, slick and snowy driveway. After parking, I grab my briefcase and sit for a few seconds. The coating of snow insulates the regular sounds of the neighborhood making for a peaceful silence disturbed only by the pinging of melting water dripping into the gutter.

Home early on Monday is a rarity. An afternoon relaxing in front of the tube, or better yet, at a bar would be perfect, but now I have obligations. Promises to keep. I open the car door and step out. My foot hits the ground and snow goes over my shoe and into my sock. I see that there's no clear path to the door, so I plow through and soak my feet.

"Daddy," welcomes me as I open the door and stomp on the outdoor mat to clear the snow off.

Sledding

Taking a step inside, I get a strong hug from my son around my leg and smell the aroma of garlic and tomatoes simmering on the stove. My wife steps out of the kitchen. "Kevin, do you know how long you two will be?"

Walking up the stairs, I yell back, "I don't plan on staying too long."

"Don't forget, we have a lot to do."

I can feel my son right behind me. In the master bedroom, I sit on the bed and take off my shoes. My son asks, "Are we going now?" from underneath a pile of snow clothes that make him look like he is wearing a burka.

I grab a pair of jeans, an old college sweatshirt and my winter boots. "Yes, right away." I throw my clothes on and head downstairs with my son again at my heels. In the kitchen, we make our promise to be home soon and are told that a warm meal will welcome us. As I am reminded again, a list of chores await. Outside, I stop to allow my eyes to adjust to the brightness of the sun reflecting off the snow.

From the car, I look back at my son. He is still at the front door staring at the snow on the ground as an insurmountable obstacle. I go back, pick him up and carry him to the backseat. I can barely feel his body through all of his clothes. Carrying him feels more like transporting a load of laundry.

After putting him in the child seat, I take us on a bumpy ride to the nearby park. I park the car, open the trunk and pull out the bright red plastic sled, water that was snow yesterday falls out of it. Taking my son's hand, I walk across the parking lot. A group of people ahead have their backs to us. Getting closer, we see them jump on their sleds and fly down the slope.

Surveying the area, I spot a steep hill that surrounds a field, which forms into a bowl; it's crowded with snowboarders, people sledding down the hill, others trudging back up and a group of people on the field building snowmen and throwing snowballs.

The kids below us are wearing an array of bright colored jackets, hats and snow pants. Against the backdrop of the white field, the clothes create the appearance of a giant bowl of living Fruity Pebbles.

I try to find an area that is free of the older aggressive kids, snow ramps, and frozen projectiles. Seeing an area off to the side, I keep Andrew's hand in mine and lead him there. I put Andrew on the sled and push him on the back. Coasting down, he holds his hands out to the sides and yells, "Full speed ahead!"

Smiling, I watch him reach the bottom and come to a stop. He sits for a few seconds, puts his hands over the side of the sled and stands up. Carrying the sled, he walks up the hill. Taking a few steps at a time, he stops and measures the remaining distance, then slowly makes it back up with the determination of Sir Edmund Hillary.

He ends up in front of me. "Daddy, come down with me this time."

Feeling my phone vibrate in my pocket, I respond, "Next time down." He sits on the sled. I position my foot in the middle of his back and push him down the hill. This time he goes faster and lets out a shriek of joy. I take out the phone and see a message from my wife. "Having fun?" I wait for Andrew to turn around with a smile on his face. I take a picture of him and hit reply.

Putting the phone in my pocket, I watch him make his way back up. When he gets to me he says, "Daddy come down with me."

"Okay." I take the sled from him, drop it on the ground, sit down on it, put my hand down to keep us steady and put him in my lap. Leaning over, I whisper into his ear, "You ready to go real fast?"

He nods. I let go of him and push off. We roll over a series of small bumps and build momentum until we reach the bottom and slide into a stop. Getting up, I turn and look at Andrew. "How was that?"

"Fun," he says as he stands up.

Sledding

Picking up the sled, I take a second to catch my breath when a person steps in front of me. I see that she clearly resembles someone from my past. She turns toward someone who calls her name. "Jackie," I hear in the distance. She looks over, smiles at the person, and goes towards her.

"Jackie" hangs in my head for a few seconds before I fully realize how much the person's face looks like my girlfriend Jackie from long ago. I continue to watch her walk off, pulling a sled behind her with two young children on it. Looking down at them, a boy and a girl, I can see her resemblance to them. I continue to stare as she fades into a crowd.

"Dad, can we go down again?" I feel a tug on my hand. Looking over to where Jackie disappeared and back to my son, I smile and try to take a step. My legs feel like they've become rooted into the ground as I watched her pass by. I pull one of them out of the snow and then the other.

At the top of the hill, I scan the crowd and pick her out. Singling her out ushers in a flood of memories. I vividly remember the night she dumped me. We were sitting on the couch of her parent's house. I leaned in to kiss her, but she turned her head and sagged forward. "We need to talk," she said as she took a deep breath and slowly let it out. "I think we should go in a different direction."

She looked back at me, pulled her hair behind her ear and stared straight ahead. "I don't feel comfortable like this anymore."

My mouth opened to respond, but nothing came out. I could feel the synapses in my brain firing, but instead of creating a connection that would deliver some sort of message, they just ricocheted inside my skull.

"The last time I saw you, I didn't feel comfortable, and now I feel the same way."

Without saying anything, I lifted my bare feet off the thick brown rug, slipped them into my leather boat shoes, got up and walked out of the room to the front door. Following behind me but at a distance, she stopped at the edge of the hallway. Opening the door, I paused. I realized where I was standing. It was where we first kissed. The world was alive with possibilities. Now, it was the place it all ended.

Her head was down and then she lifted it, looked directly into my eyes and said, "Sorry." I turned and walked out of the house.

Later that night, when I was finally able to get the messages in my brain to form in my mouth, I must have tried to call her twenty times with no answer. What was I going to say? How was I going to convince her to change her mind? Playing those scenes over in my mind, I feel like the director of a play that yells cut at the actors, but they continue rehearsing the same scenes over and over again.

"Daddy, let's go down the hill again," I hear from below. I drop the sled on the ground and look back over to where I saw Jackie. I can't believe she's here. I haven't seen her in years. Do I go over there and talk to her? Ignoring her isn't right but talking to her would be awkward. Would she be happy to see me or would it just be uncomfortable? It would probably be uncomfortable. The easiest thing would be to avoid her.

"Dad, let's go down again."

"Hold on a second, Andrew." Maybe I should just tell him we need to leave.

"Daddy, what are you waiting for?"

"Why don't you go down by yourself this time?"

"I want you to come with me."

She's on the other side of the park now. I can stay out of her line of sight, go down a few more times and take off.

"Daddy, I'm waiting."

"Okay, Andrew." I sit, put him in my lap and slide back down. Standing up, I don't see her. As I'm heading back up the hill, I find her breaking away from a crowd and walking across the field.

We dated for more than three years throughout high school

Sledding

and college. We had our lives all planned out. We would graduate and get married. We even knew the church, the wedding party and where we would have the reception, but, one day, that all crashed to the ground.

My son sits down in the sled. Pausing for a second, I remember the last time I saw Jackie. It was at a friend's wedding after we broke up. We were alone and she stared right at me, leaned into me, but this time I turned away. Why did I do that? I wanted so bad to have her back. Was I somehow exacting revenge? How many times has that moment crossed my mind? How many times have I regretted it?

Jarred by the sound of my son banging on the sled, I look down at Andrew. He taps the sled again to signal me to sit down. I watch Jackie. She seems to be walking to the other side of the park. By the time I go down, I should be clear of her field of vision. I smile at Andrew, sit behind him and push us down. We slide to a stop, turn and stand up. Jackie is in front of me; she stopped to tie her kid's shoelace. She lifts her head and looks right at me. Stopping for a second, we stare at each other. "Jackie?" I say.

I watch her as she pieces my identity together. "Kevin?" she says as she pops up, runs toward me and engulfs me in a hug. The force of the embrace makes me take several steps backward. I catch myself and try to pull away from her, but she holds onto me. "I can't believe I ran into you here," she says as she lets go.

"I thought you moved to Chicago," I say.

"I did but with my divorce I thought it would be better to get a fresh start."

Divorce? Did she say she got divorced? I hadn't known that. Last I heard she was married with kids. She continues, "How about you? What are you up to?"

I fumble for words. "Lot of time at work. Keeps me busy."

"Yeah, you've always been a hard worker. Mister straight A's," she says as she gives me a friendly punch in the arm.

"How about you? Are you just back in the area?" I say.

"Yeah, just staying with friends now but going to find a place, a job and get to know people." As she speaks I see something different in her. She isn't what I remember. In my memory she's imprisoned as a person in her early twenties that hasn't aged or matured. All of her youthful mannerisms are gone. She's grown up.

"You live near here?" she asks me.

"Yeah, just over in that neighborhood," I say pointing into the distance.

"Jackie?" One of her friends calls to her and points to her watch.

Jackie grabs my arm and says, "I have to leave, but we should get together. Let me give you my cell." I pull out my phone and take down her number. She gives me another hug and runs over to catch up to her friends.

I stand watching her join her group. Continuing to walk, she says something to the person next to her, turns, and smiles at me. When she does, I remember the first time I met her at a party. She was the prettiest of the group of girls she was with, and I walked away with her.

I never got over her. Somewhere in my dreams, we never broke up and I've been unable to let go of that fantasy. Now, it could all be true. We could be together again. I look down at the number in my phone. All I would have to do is call her.

I feel something pulling my leg. I get down on my knee so I'm at his eye level. "Who was that?" He asks. To myself I say that is the first person to break my heart. She's the one that taught me that not all of our dreams come true.

"Just an old friend that I haven't seen in a long time."

We both turn toward Jackie, who is walking away. When she broke up with me, she crushed me. I didn't want to give my heart to anyone again. I thought she was the only one in the world for me and that I would never be able to fully give myself to anyone

Sledding

for fear of having my heart broken like that again.

I turn back to Andrew's deep blue eyes. My married life flashes before me. I remember the first time I saw Emily. Right there somehow I knew that I wanted to spend the rest of my life with her. I see myself on one knee proposing. She was crying so hard, she couldn't get out her answer. Images of our wedding run through my head like a slide show.

I see myself holding Andrew for the first time and having more love for him than for anyone or anything. I picture myself sitting on the edge of our bed when I had to tell my wife I lost my first job. I was embarrassed and humiliated. I was terrified of how long I would be out of work. She took my hand and said, "No matter what happens we'll get through this together."

As all of this fires through my brain, I realize I've been wrong. Jackie wasn't the person imprisoned in my memory. I was. I trapped myself in a fantasy and have been stuck with the notion that some other life might be better. I get so caught up in the day to day life of working, being a husband, a father and everything that goes along with it somehow I lost track of how much I already have.

Andrew wipes his nose, "Dad?"

"Yes, Andrew."

"I'm cold. "I want to see Mommy and have some hot chocolate and paghetti." He always leaves off the "s" in "spaghetti."

"Do you miss Mommy?" I ask him.

He nods. I turn, look back to where Jackie was, and back to him. "Me too." I reach down to my phone and delete Jackie's number.

Hand in hand, we walk back to the car.

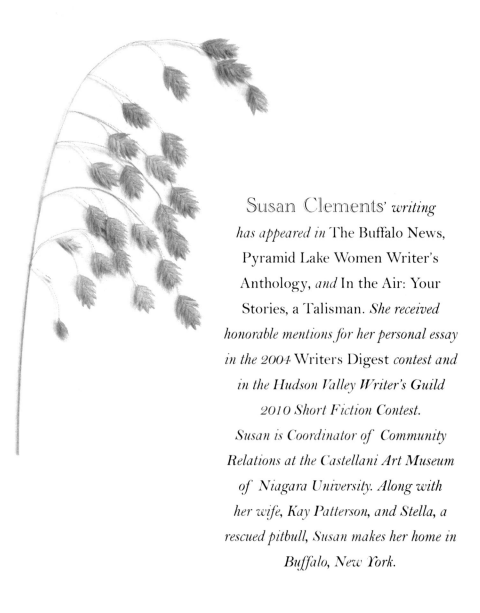

Susan Clements' *writing has appeared in* The Buffalo News, Pyramid Lake Women Writer's Anthology, *and* In the Air: Your Stories, a Talisman. *She received honorable mentions for her personal essay in the 2004* Writers Digest *contest and in the Hudson Valley Writer's Guild 2010 Short Fiction Contest. Susan is Coordinator of Community Relations at the Castellani Art Museum of Niagara University. Along with her wife, Kay Patterson, and Stella, a rescued pitbull, Susan makes her home in Buffalo, New York.*

Manatee Mornings

Susan Clements

Fiction

Christie imagines herself a manatee, gliding silently through the warm gulf waters, nibbling on fronds of kelp, avoiding the danger of boat propellers and water intakes. She is graceful, weightless, an underwater athlete despite her bulk. Tourists lean over the railings of their tour boats to take her picture. "Look, how beautiful!" Snap, snap, snap. She is the sea creature that sailors mistook for a mermaid. How easily she glides in this blue world.

Christie is swimming laps in the least used pool of the Bel Aire Palms resort. She likes this pool because it is tucked away behind some conveniently tall shrubbery and a thick stand of palmettos. She has to walk around the back of the miniature golf course and cut through a disused wing of the hotel to get to it—her own personal pool.

She's been coming first thing in the morning since she discovered it three days ago. No one has disturbed her routine thus far. She swims a slow, deliberate crawl. She could swim forever, slow and easy, like Gertrude Ederle who greased her body with lard and swam the icy English Channel. She's strong enough. She has the endurance. Christie would rather be a manatee.

As she reaches the end of lap number forty-eight, Christie sees two legs dangling in the water. Pale, bony knees, and chartreuse water shoes. An intruder! Christie will ignore this person until he or she—no, it's a she, the legs are hairless—goes away. On to lap forty-nine and fifty. She always stops at fifty. Maybe a few more. She can swim forever.

"These old bones are a mass of calcification today," Fern thinks as she dips her foot into the water. "Ooh, that's a little 'invigoratin' as Pop used to say. No matter. I'll calcify completely if I don't get in there and move around some." She moves down to the second step, and then the third, bending to splash water on her upper arms. A last step down into the pool, and the water reaches her pendulous breasts. She gasps a little, "That's the worst part over then." The water isn't so bad, now that she's in it. She pulls her bathing cap over her wispy white hair and commences some arm exercises. Back and forth, back and forth, up and down, up and down. Have to keep moving, no matter what.

Fern is a little annoyed that she's not alone in the pool. Today is her first day back from the rehab center, and she was looking forward to easing back into her routine with a little privacy. It's bad enough that she has to use a cane, what with the osteoporosis and a mended hip. Now the damned tourists have discovered her pool. Why can't they stick to the one with the bar and the waterslide? This one doesn't even have a bathroom nearby. Good thing her condo is just across the way.

Manatee Mornings

"Lord, that woman swims like a machine, back and forth. Look at the size of her. Good swimmer, though," she thinks. "I used to be able to swim like that." She remembers when she swam in the ocean every day. Their house at the beach. She remembers her friend, gone ten years. "Come on Fern, move those arms, you'll freeze into one position like the tin man." Her knee chooses this moment to lock up.

Rae peers between the palmettos and wraps her terrycloth robe tightly around herself. She could have sworn there was no one around when she spotted the deserted pool from her tenth floor window. She set out to find it only to be waylaid by a maze of koi ponds, golf carts and gazebos. Now it's crawling with people. Two, to be exact. An old lady in one of those quilted bathing caps with a big rubber rose on it, and a hefty woman swimming laps at a glacial pace. She never makes a splash, not even when she comes to the wall, lifts her head and fixes Rae with a decidedly hostile look. The old lady spots her too, and raises a claw-like hand in greeting.

Rae slinks back to her hotel room and her stack of John Grisham novels.

"A walking skeleton," thinks Fern. "Good lord."

Wednesday morning, first thing, Christie heads down to the pool. Everyone else is at the all-you-can-eat breakfast buffet, but Christie wants to get her laps in before company arrives. She is feeling a little more fit every day. Her breathing is easier, not so much huffing and puffing trying to keep up with everybody else. The long winters up north are getting harder to take. Seems like she hibernates half the year, barely moving from November to May.

She is not alone. A slender woman is ensconced in a lounge chair in the corner. Her eyes are hidden behind opaque sunglasses, and she appears to be engrossed in one of those popular paperbacks you get at the airport.

Christie was looking forward to a good bask before plunging in, but she's not about to expose her expanse of flesh to someone who looks like *that*. She will sit in one of the upright chairs at the other end, just for a minute or two, in her cover-up. She tries not to stare at the woman in the orange bikini, but a few furtive glances reveal that the woman is more than model thin. When she leans over to get sunscreen out of her tote, Christie can see her spine outlined like a garden hose under a Slip 'N Slide®. "Must be anorexic." Christie shudders inwardly and looks away.

The silent swimmer slips into the water like a seal from an ice floe. "She hates me," thinks Rae. She knows that look—the one she gets from other women. Like they want to slap her silly. Eat, you skinny moron! If only they knew. In her marathon days, she consumed mountains of pasta before each race. Carbohydrate packing, they called it. At first she ran to keep off the freshman fifteen, and then she grew to like it. Soon she was competing in 5Ks and running ten miles a day, rain or shine. On days she couldn't run, she felt agitated and depressed at the same time. By the time she graduated from college, Rae had run her first marathon. She'd begun lifting weights and at one point could bench press over a hundred pounds. She ran so much her body began to resemble that of a concentration camp survivor, muscles wasting away when there was no fat left to burn.

One morning, Rae woke up and didn't have the urge to run anymore. At thirty-two, her chest was concave, both feet had stress fractures and she could barely lift her head from the pillow.

Manatee Mornings

Distraught husband Mark has carted her off to this seaside resort for rest and recuperation. She is under doctor's orders not to run. She has no desire to. She only wants to bake in the sun like an iguana and forget everything including Dr. Chaudri, Eileen, her therapist, and especially Mark and his worried look. She'd rather put up with *Shamu* over their glaring at her.

Fern is feeling more herself every day, the rehab center fading to an uncherished memory. She feels like the bionic woman lately, with more replacement parts than originals. She wonders how much longer she can go on before she'll have to give up the condo and move into one of those assisted living centers. Worse yet, the kids up in snow country are making noises about her moving in with them. She wants to postpone that as long as possible. She loves her daughter, but they just can't get along. Fern has too many ideas about how a household should be run, and Patricia is acting irrational these days.

She gives a little thank you to the God she doesn't really believe in each morning that she wakes up and can still haul herself up onto her feet. She knows her days of independence are numbered, and she's got to keep moving no matter how much her bones ache. Better this than camp out in perimenopausal Pattie's spare room.

This morning, Fern has brought her water exercise balls. She begins by gripping the handles and pulling them straight down into the water. It's harder than it used to be. Better not overdo it. One slips from her grasp and rockets into the air, landing with a splash right in front of the lap swimmer's face. Uh-oh.

The errant projectile is silently returned to her.

"Sorry, honey," says Fern, "It got away from me." The woman cracks a tiny smile. "You're quite the swimmer."

"It helps that I float like a cork," says Christie, smiling for real this time.

At the salad bar, Christie is trying to decide between the local Italian (probably disgusting, but virtuous) and the "lite" ranch. What she really wants is the creamy bleu cheese and some of that nice, hot French bread. Maybe she'll have the bleu cheese and do some more laps later. It sure beats going shopping again. What is with these people, anyway? Maryanne, the nonstop talker in the group, hasn't gone to the beach once. Why would you spend the money on a plane ticket when all you want to do is smoke, drink and spend money on hideous trinkets? Oh yeah, and flirt with every waiter who puts a plate in front of you. She's had about enough of Maryanne. Christie spots someone familiar as she returns to her table. It's that skinny person from the pool. She's leaning up against a big, nice looking guy in a fuchsia t-shirt that says "Life's a Beach." His hair is black and shiny like a mink's pelt. He's jabbering away, and she's just staring off into space, chomping away on a big burger. She's working on a pile of fries too. Christie decides looks can be deceiving.

The late afternoon sun casts purple shadows across the deep end of the pool. Calm has descended on the Bel Aire Palms. The absence of screaming kids and splashing means people have gone off to get ready for dinner. The air is heavy with humidity and birdsong.

Rae is dozing in the corner lounge, dreaming of the New York Marathon. She's running smooth and steady, in the zone, no pain in her feet, just that runner's high. Without warning, the pavement opens up and she's falling into a bottomless abyss, legs pumping furiously. She awakes with a jerk and realizes she's been drooling, sits up and rubs at the crick in her neck. Everything hurts.

Someone is waving at her from a balcony across the street. It's that old lady from earlier today, and she's out there waving at her with—what—a fly swatter? No, a spatula. Rae waves back.

Mark must be back from the golf course by now. Rae gathers her things and makes her way slowly back to the room, calculating how much time there is to get through before she can sleep again.

"How many?" Fern asks as Christie removes her goggles and shakes the water out of her ears. "Sixty-two," she says, slightly out of breath, but feeling rather proud of herself. This is getting to be a routine. Christie swims, and Fern demands to know how many laps.

"Good girl, you keep that up," says Fern.

Rae has been eavesdropping. It's better than a tranquilizer, listening to Fern go on and on. Between laps, Fern tells Christie about her broken hip and her recent "incarceration" at the rehab center, makes recommendations on sites to see and places to eat. She's a virtual Frommer's. And that Christie isn't so bad, really. She has a nice, melodic voice that's soothing to the ear. Neither of them has asked, "Are you all right?" like Mark does every five minutes. It's therapeutic, lying here being ignored. It feels like the boundaries of the world end at the palmettos.

Christie settles into a lounge chair and sighs. Only three more days and its back to work. The sun feels so good on her skin. To hell with sunscreen. She wants to go back with a tan to taunt her coworkers. Fern is holding on to the ladder, doing a series of leg lifts. That old woman never stops moving. She hears a soft splash.

"Getting too hot for you?" says Fern. Christie opens her eyes and sees that Rae is in the water, doing a nearly vertical breaststroke. No fat to keep her legs up at all.

"Yeah, it's a hot all right," says Rae. "Water feels good." This is the first thing that's felt good in a long time.

Shawna has been wandering around the resort for half an hour, trying to find the site for the shoot. Good thing she came a day early to scout it out. It would be *so* embarrassing to look like she doesn't know what she's doing on her first assignment. Shawna works for the ad agency that handles the Bel Aire Palms' account. They want the smaller pool included in the new brochures for next year, when the Cocoa Palm wing reopens. She's got the photographer and models all lined up. Now it's just a matter of figuring out the logistics and deciding which angles to shoot. Where the heck is this place? She's starting to get frustrated when she spots the closed down wing. Oh good, she can have the crew park in that development right across the street. Much easier! The pool itself is surrounded by a lot of dense foliage. Oh well, they can play that up in the ad copy. "*Honeymooners will enjoy this romantic, secluded hideaway...*"

Shawna jots these ideas on her clipboard as she approaches the pool.

"Hello ladies!" she chirps. These people will have to go somewhere else tomorrow. One looks like a bag of bones, the other one is as big as a house, and the old one is waving around these weird looking things that look like boobs with handles. This is not the image the Bel Aire Palms wants to project.

She plunges in. "I'm Shawna Parker from Pavilion Advertising, and I wanted to let you know we're going to be doing a photo shoot here tomorrow for the resort."

"Oh goodie," says Fern. "We'll be famous."

"Actually," says Shawna, "we'll be using *professional models* for the shoot. But you're welcome to watch from over there," she adds, pointing beyond the palmettos. She's the queen of diplomacy.

Manatee Mornings

Fern gets a little twinkle in her eye. "We'd be happy to pose for free, won't we?"

From the corner comes a snort.

Shawna is momentarily struck speechless. "O-kay. Well, then. That's *very* sweet, but we've got our *own* people—*professionals*. Soooo...okay, then, I'll be back *tomorrow*, with the *photographer*, and the *models*, and it won't take long, *really*..."

Christie submerges, drowning a rude retort.

"I'll wear my best Sunday swimsuit," says Fern.

Shawna beats a hasty retreat.

"Twerp," says Christie.

"You got that right," says Rae.

Christie arrives earlier than usual the next day in order to get her laps in before the photo crew arrives. She's planning to make herself scarce when the hard bodies show up. It's pretty obvious that Little Miss Ad Agency with her pert blonde ponytail and tan legs doesn't want someone like Christie featured in the brochure. Christie isn't exactly eager to be photographed in her all of her ample glory either. She's surprised to see Rae already installed in the corner lounge. A few minutes later Fern arrives, resplendent in a lime green floral mumu.

The morning's peaceful routine is soon interrupted by the arrival of the photographer, a rangy guy with dreadlocks and a Hawaiian shirt, Shawna with clipboard in hand, and six models. There's a preppy, young white couple, a hip, thirty-something black couple, and two incredibly trim and youthful-looking seniors. The man has a mane of perfectly coiffed, silvery hair and a deep tan. The woman looks like an advertisement for botox injections. Christie has never seen so many perfect teeth in one place. She'll just finish this one lap and get out of their way.

"How many?" demands Fern, scuttling over like a crab.
"Forty-five," says Christie.
"Good girl, you keep going," says Fern.
"But they're getting ready to..."
"That's okay, honey, you just keep going." Fern gives Christie a mischievous look. She's up to something, and Christie thinks she knows what it is. A swim-in? Okay, then. Let them wait for her to finish. She only has five laps to go.

"Excuse me," says Shawna, walking along the edge of the pool as Christie swims. "Ex-*cuse* me! Miss! Miss!" Christie keeps on swimming. Forty-seven, forty-eight... Shawna sticks to Christie like Gertrude Ederle's escort boat.

In the meantime, Fern has struck up a conversation with Roy, the photographer. She wants to know how he gets his hair to do that.

Christie hits the wall, and Fern says, "How many?"
"Fifty," she says, "and now I'm going to..."
"Keep going, honey, you can do it." Fern's look is a command. Christie shrugs and pushes off again.

Shawna feels a scream coming on. That big gal won't stop swimming, and the old lady is starting to do exercises in the middle of the pool, and she's paying these models by the hour. Okay, focus, start with something easy. Some background shots.

Rae is watching events unfold with amusement.

"Excuse me?" It's the ad agency person. "Do you think you could move over there? We want to take a few shots of this area."

Rae emits a tubercular cough. "I'm not supposed to move around a lot," she says. "Doctor's orders." She tries to look even weaker than she feels.

"Excuse me, I'll be right back." Shawna escapes through the opening in the shrubbery.

"Where ya going, honey? We're all ready for you!" bellows Fern.

Manatee Mornings

"Rita? This is Shawna. From Pavilion? Can you come over here for a minute? I've got a *situation*." Thank God Rita picked up. The resort's assistant manager is a seasoned pro. She'll know how to get rid of these people.

Rita takes her time strolling over. This Shawna person is a double pain in the ass. She has better things to do than babysit a novice. Rita arrives just as the old lady has coaxed three of the models into the pool and is demonstrating the uses of exercise balls. The corpse in the corner is humming, "We're on the island of misfit toys..." and the swimmer keeps on swimming.

"How many?" says Fern as Christie breaks the surface, gasping for air.

"Sixty-three..."

"Good girl. Just a few more, that's right."

Christie thinks her lungs might explode.

"Hello Fern," says Rita, plopping herself down in a nearby chair. "How's it going?"

"We're helping this nice young lady out."

"I can see that." Rita leans back and lights up a Newport. Geez, it's hot today. "You're looking spry," she says, crossing one varicose-veined leg over the other.

"Exercise, exercise, keeps me young," says Fern. "You should try it sometime." Rita expels a sharp bark of amusement.

"Well, enjoy." Rita motions with her head for the wet-behind-the-ears kid to follow her. Out of earshot, she says, "You see that old lady? That's Fern. She doesn't even stay at our property, but she threatened to sue us when we tried to stop her from using this pool every goddamn day. She'll have NewsCenter Six down here in five minutes flat if you keep this up. So here's what you're gonna do. Shoot around 'em."

Uncertain Promise

"But…" Rita cuts off Shawna's protest with a steely glare. With that, she takes a good long drag on her cigarette and saunters off, leaving Shawna to figure the rest out for herself.

Roy is packing up his camera and the models have gone back to the van. Shawna departs with a flounce of her ponytail. "Later," says Roy.

Christie floats on her back, gazing up at the palm trees.

"How many?" says Fern.

"One hundred and four," says Christie. "How many did *you* do?"

"I wasn't counting."

Rae can't remember when she laughed so hard.

Another raw November afternoon, and it's raining again. Christie hates these short, dark days. She stomps up the stairs and grabs the mail. Bills, more bills, credit card offers and something colorful—a brochure from the Bel Air Palms. She goes through the house flipping lights on in every room. The cat is circling her legs, screeching for food, but she ignores him. She's remembering sunshine and clear blue water.

Near the back of the glossy booklet, sure enough, there's her pool. There's the honeymooners, the black couple and the sporty seniors. But no Fern. No Christie, no Rae. Of course not.

Something catches her eye, something that's not supposed to be there. The honeymoon couple is shown playing a frisky game of tag. In the space between pursuing hubby and laughing, fleeing wife, Christie spots a familiar shape bobbing in the background. She wonders how Shawna missed that exercise ball.

Manatee Mornings

She smiles when she sees the shadow on the bottom of the bright blue pool. A shadow shaped like a manatee.

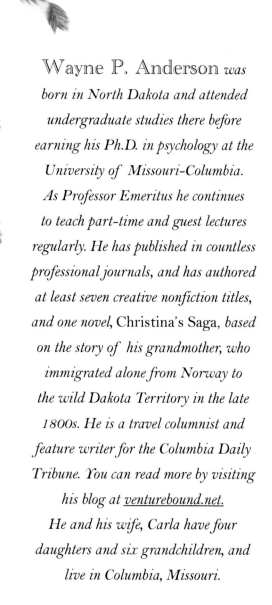

Wayne P. Anderson *was born in North Dakota and attended undergraduate studies there before earning his Ph.D. in psychology at the University of Missouri-Columbia. As Professor Emeritus he continues to teach part-time and guest lectures regularly. He has published in countless professional journals, and has authored at least seven creative nonfiction titles, and one novel,* Christina's Saga, *based on the story of his grandmother, who immigrated alone from Norway to the wild Dakota Territory in the late 1800s. He is a travel columnist and feature writer for the Columbia Daily Tribune. You can read more by visiting his blog at <u>venturebound.net.</u>*

He and his wife, Carla have four daughters and six grandchildren, and live in Columbia, Missouri.

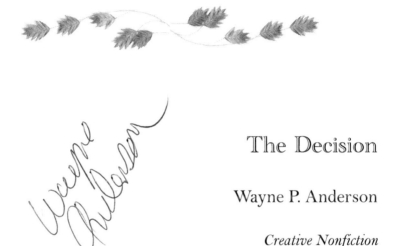

The Decision

Wayne P. Anderson

Creative Nonfiction

My legs felt like tree trunks; my arms refused to respond to messages from my brain. My muscles were aching; my head was throbbing. A steady pain somewhere behind my eyes made it hard for me to look directly at anything. But it was the dehydration that was killing me. Bundles of wheat lay in a large depression where no breeze would come to ease the 105-degree heat. Disgusted at the willpower required to move, I built a large shock of wheat, pulled myself into its shade, and sat staring at the hole working its way through the knee of my jeans. Whiskey shots and beer chasers the night before had done their mischief.

David, my boss and the owner of the farm, had dropped me off in a wheat field over which he had run the binder the day before. He had left me a burlap-covered jug of water and a sack lunch. "This field should keep you busy 'til late afternoon," he told me. "I'll come back to pick you up. If you get done early, walk over to the other field. I'll be cutting there."

Deep inside, I heard a voice screaming. "There's got to be a better way to live than this. I hate heat. I hate pain. I hate work."

Most of us make decisions every day—little ones, big ones. But when I graduated from high school in 1947—seventeen years old with no serious plan for the future other than to get a job and earn a living—I had made no real decisions as to what my future would be. If there was an internal compass pointing the way to my future, I didn't know I had it. I had no idea that the decision that would shape my life was still a year away.

My odyssey into the hell of hard manual labor began when I found work helping to rebuild a large power plant. This was before the days of heavy machinery that could work in confined areas; human muscle power was still the best way to move dirt and debris. When I signed on, the pit crew had already broken up the foundation of the old plant. Working at the bottom of the resulting hole, our job was to dig into the rock and shale, to lift it onto a conveyor belt that carried it to dump trucks above. Noise from jackhammers and other machines made talking impossible. We sang at the top of our lungs; we hollered obscenities at the foreman. But no one heard. In the dust, and heat, and darkness, we were alone, each of us in his private inferno. Foremen on platforms overhead watched us. Anyone who paused too long or too frequently received a pink slip at the end of the week. Occasionally, some unfortunate was called out of the pit and fired on the spot. Though not quite slaves on a Roman galley, our condition seemed at times little better.

Motivated by a mother and a younger brother I was helping to support, gifted with youth and in good physical condition, I lasted longer than most. Several hundred men passed through the job in

The Decision

the four months I was there. But in time I got fired. By then I felt as though they had cheated me, had given me a shovel that grew heavier and heavier, day by day. Finally, they gave me one I could barely lift. Funny thing was, it looked just like the one I had been using all along.

Dismissed from the power plant, I found work with a railroad—dangerous work repairing bridges. My brother Huck, twenty years older than I, was a crane operator with them, and I had high hopes of working my way up. But again, I stayed only a short while. Someone in the head office decided my eyes were too weak and insisted that I be let go. If my glasses fell off, the other guys could be at hazard. I then went back to Jensen, my contact at the U. S. Employment Service, who told me a group from Missouri was hiring men to harvest June grass. "June grass," he said in response to my puzzled look, "it's what they use for grass seed in the stores."

And so, I climbed into my venerable 1931 Plymouth and headed across the prairie figuring that working with a pitchfork turning over grass could not be much different from handling a shovel. I knew my hands were calloused enough for that.

Working at the power plant, I had come to believe that many of my co-workers were not of the highest caliber—drifters, alcoholics, misfits, hard cases of every description. Among the June buggers, I found some of the men were worse. At the time I thought of them as "real men"—though my idea of a "real man" was admittedly limited. To fit in you had to be able to drink excessively, even to unconsciousness. You had to fuck once in a while, but buying it was OK, and you had to not back down from a fight. Because of my youth I expected a certain amount of hazing. What I wasn't prepared for was the cruelty directed at some of the most defenseless.

For a while the group's victim was Gormer. His clothes were more ragged than those the rest of us wore; he actually had a knotted clothesline rope for a belt. The way his clothes hung on him, he seemed once to have been a larger man who was gradually shrinking into nothingness, folding in on himself. He claimed to be a veteran who had seen combat, but his tormentors doubted that since they couldn't imagine anyone dumb enough to trust him with a gun. Walking a row, turning over the grass, we could talk to the next man down the line—but no one wanted that next man to be Gormer whose movements were dangerously jerky and mechanical and who talked to himself constantly.

"No, no, that's not the way it happened," he said to no one in particular one day when I was within earshot.

"What happened?" I asked.

"He said I was a coward. He said I shit my pants when we tried to take the ruins."

"Who said?"

"Clyde. That was Clyde."

"Who's Clyde, Gormer?"

"Clyde, my friend Clyde. He talks to me. He keeps me company now."

With that, Gormer turned away, mumbling to himself about the friend only he could see. Back then I didn't know the term "auditory hallucination." To us Gormer was simply "crazy as a bedbug."

"Tell me about Clyde, Gormer," I asked, hoping to understand.

"Clyde was my buddy. We was at Anzio together. The Germans beat the shit out of us. Then we fought at a mountain with a castle on it. Our B-17s bombed it to hell, but the Germans still had the high ground, and they lobbed shells down on us."

Gormer stopped working. He looked in my direction, but with that "thousand yard stare" that suggested he didn't see me at all. I had a weird feeling, but shook it off and asked, "What happened?"

The Decision

Gormer's eyes came into focus and met mine. "One of the shells hit Clyde in the head. I had his head all over me. I had his brains on my face."

He stopped talking, glared at me as if he dared me to contradict what he had said. I stared back, fascinated by what he was saying.

"After we took the pass, I was sent back to rest. After I got some sleep and a good meal or two, Clyde showed up and started talking to me. I get mad at him and tell him he's dead and to go away, but he just keeps coming back."

"Do you hear him in your head? Can you see him?"

A pause, he seemed to be listening. "Clyde says I shouldn't talk about him. He's nobody's business but mine. Now leave me alone."

Working alongside Mort, accepted by the rest of the veterans on the crew as an authentic hero, I asked him about Gormer's story. Mort gave me that fuzzy look he often had when nursing a bottle in his tent. "He's all fucked up in the brain. His stories don't make no sense. I was in Italy; I know the units that fought there. He don't have his facts straight."

But Gormer's tortured mind didn't stop the others from abusing him. On occasion they'd come up behind Gormer and shout "BANG" or "incoming" for the perverse pleasure of seeing him jump. Their pleasure, his pain. Once in a while—to their delight—he'd even hit the ground. One day he just wasn't there anymore.

Appleberry, the owner of the outfit, had a live-in girlfriend, Essie May, who worked as cook for the crew. Despite her "advanced age"—she was in her mid-thirties—I found her more than attractive and, perhaps, envied Appleberry just a bit. He wasn't nearly so appreciative. We would hear them screaming at each other at night, until one morning she emerged from the house with a black eye and just took off. The most trustworthy guy in the bunch, I cooked while she was away—fried potatoes, beans and franks every night, another kind of cruelty. But after a week, Essie May returned to the delight of the workers. After a few days the night time arguments returned, but I heard no more slaps or blows.

As the youngest member of the crew I had my own lessons to learn. Tolson—the field foreman, a character straight from central casting—had a shock of white hair and deep lines descending from his nose to his mouth that gave him a bulldog look. Even during the summer he wore long underwear under his plaid cotton shirt, the underarms and back heavy with white salt stains. He said the extra layer absorbed heat and the sweat kept him cooler. Tolson was a snuff dipper who could spit a stream of brown juice with uncanny accuracy. I once saw him hit a grasshopper at ten paces. A hole was worn in his overall's back pocket where he kept his Copenhagen.

One day, hearing me complain about the heat, he stepped closer and twisted off the cap of the Copenhagen. "I got just what you need, Andy. Take a pinch, put it under your lip, and in a few minutes you won't mind the heat at all."

I took a pinch, put it under my lip and went back to turning grass. Minutes later, the field and the men around me began moving in strange ways. The scene spun around; I felt myself falling into a pit. Next thing I knew someone was dripping water over my face. Waking, the first thing I saw was Tolson's bulldog smile above my head.

"Guess you ain't ready to join the men yet," he said. Pleased at having taken me down a step or two, he turned to a couple of other men, "Blue, Boney, see that Andy gets to his tent. I don't think he'll be much good for a couple of hours."

Trying to blend in with the group was not always easy. If someone questioned your manhood, the unwritten rule was that you had to be willing to fight to keep your place in the pecking order. George, short and not very heavy, with a swagger in his walk, learned of my reputation as a boxer and challenged me.

"Anderson, I hear you're a real tough guy."

The Decision

"That's what they tell me. You wanna try me?" My response was the only one possible. And given his size, I figured I could beat the shit out of him. I handed my glasses to someone in the crowd that had gathered, hoping for a little blood, and I took a boxer's stance. I was expecting the usual kind of fight where you square off and go after each other with fists.

The next thing I knew I was flat on my back in a pile of grass. George had his knees on my arms and was whaling away with both fists, pummeling my face. Tolson and Blue pulled him off before he completely destroyed me. I figured later that he got me out of action so fast by kicking my feet out from under me, dropping on my stomach with his knees to wind me, and with me helpless proceeded to shoot my reputation all to hell.

When the June grass season was over, I worked on farms shocking grain and doing odd jobs with two other June buggers, Frank and Boney. Like Gormer, Frank was a veteran of the war in Europe whose mind had been twisted by too many days and months in combat. He was also a psychopath of the first order. His post-war claim to fame was that he had seen the inside of a jail in every state in the Union. Food wasn't important to Frank. Whatever money he made was spent on whores and booze—and he would drink anything likely to get him drunk. One time I saw him strain hair tonic through bread and pour it down his throat. I went along with the life style, even to the point of stealing gas from tractors at night so there would be more money for alcohol. I wasn't on a good track, and deep inside I knew it.

And then, my life changed. After an epic night of drinking, Frank and Boney took off in my car for another job leaving me at David's farm where I had been shocking wheat. Though I never saw them again, I did in time recover my car, deserted and with the engine burned out. Looking back, it occurs to me now that I was more than a little like that car—burned out. That was when I found myself sitting in David's field, clinging to the meager shade of the shock of wheat I had thrown together with the last of my energy, too hungover to work. Wallowing in self-pity, I heard that voice inside my head.

"There's got to be a better way to live than this. I hate heat. I hate pain. I hate work. My pals are interesting, but some have more than a few shortcomings." The voice went on.

"Why don't you go to college?"

"College? Nobody in my family has ever gone to college."

"Yes, but people who go to college don't have to work for a living. They wear white shirts and get to take a bath every week. They don't have to work out in the hot sun. Go to college."

And suddenly, it was done. I had made the decision.

"You didn't get much done. I'll have to bring you back tomorrow." David had returned to pick me up, and he was none too pleased with my lack of progress. Evidently, he didn't notice that in the hours he had been gone, I had grown into a different person—a college student, a man with a future. I looked at him carefully. He seemed the same. But me? How could he miss the difference? Realizing that explaining how far I had traveled since morning would be impossible, my reply to David was short—and evasive.

"You sure this is only 12 acres?"

Having decided to go to college, I had no idea what to do next, only a naïve faith that someone at the college in Jamestown would have answers to my questions. Had I known how many problems lay ahead of me, I might not have gone forward. Sometimes ignorance really is bliss. I earned a bachelor's degree and fell madly in love with a wonderful woman who agreed to marry me—and support

The Decision

me while I earned a master's degree and a Ph.D. If, that is, I would do the same for her when I finished with school. She did; I did. Together we raised four children—the perfect number on which we had agreed before marrying, and under the same terms of sharing household duties in the process. With a degree in counseling psychology, I went to work at a Veterans' Administration hospital, specializing in the rehabilitation of men like Frank and Gormer who suffered from service-related mental problems. Later, I returned to the university and taught for thirty-two years. For fifteen years after "retiring," I trained teachers, mental health workers and doctors to work with traumatized children in places like Bosnia and Pakistan. I became a travel writer and am still writing books.

Hard to believe, even for me, that it all began one day in a blisteringly hot field of wheat when, unable or unwilling to go on, determined suddenly to change the direction of my life, I made "the decision."

CPSIA information can be obtained
at www.ICGtesting.com
Printed in the USA
FFOW02n1008011214
9127FF